S0-BSM-342

William L. Coleman

HARVEST HOUSE PUBLISHERS
Eugene, Oregon 97402

BOUNCING BACK

Copyright © 1985 by Harvest House Publishers
Eugene, Oregon 97402

Library of Congress Catalog Card Number 84-82350
Trade edition ISBN 0-89081-455-4
Mass edition ISBN 0-89081-531-3

Printed in the United States of America.

Thanks for the Help!

Many people have given their encouragement, advice, and illustrations as this book came together. I want to give special appreciation to those listed below and to those whose names I've forgotten.

Paul Welter
John Wilcox
Julie Meyer
Dan and Joy Straley
Alice Hixson
Doug Bildt
Don and Lois Larson
Dave Larson
Cliff and Jessie Jensen
Steve and Cheryl Roberts

Keep Getting Up!

We all know people who seem to get knocked down more than their share. They've had health problems, money trouble, lost love, job setbacks, and termite invasions. Yet each time they shake the dust off, pull in their belts, and come up smiling.

These are the people who can face rejection, learn from it, and keep going. What are their secrets? How do they gain their balance? Where do they find the courage to bounce back and climb higher than ever?

Most of us would like to get a handle on rejection. This book is written to help sift out facts from fiction, to help understand what's happening and what we can do about it. It also reminds us that God would like to lend a hand and give us an added bounce.

Bill Coleman
Aurora, Nebraska

CONTENTS

1

Everyone Gets
Knocked Down

It isn't fun to have your legs knocked out from under you. But it happens to everyone.

The talented, the rich, the beautiful, the healthy—all are rejected sooner or later. We're insulted, fired, divorced, ignored, defeated, devalued, and abandoned. It's the human condition.

In our fantasies we often dream of living above the darts of life. However, it is one dream that's hardly worth the effort. There is no beauty without ugliness. There is no creativity without pain. There is no glory without agony. There is no victory without sacrifice.

Once we accept these cliches as facts, we can begin to live more easily with rejection. We begin to turn rejection into a positive force.

Those who spend their talents trying to avoid rejection are wasting their abilities. They begin to build forts to defend themselves. They start hiding to escape conflict. Soon they go out of their way to sidestep new encounters. That person is in the battle of life, but he spends his time ducking, dodging, and covering up.

The smart person learns to accept rejection and looks for ways to turn it into a creative force. Life is filled with happiness, joy, and fulfillment. In fact, most of our dreams *do* come true; only a few of our dreams are discarded. Unfortunately, it is the few disappointments which catch our attention.

A successful businessman recently said he faced rejection continuously. However, he felt the key to success was to keep steadily at the task. Eventually dripping water will wear away rock. We cannot allow rejection to set us into a spin that ultimately leads to a crash.

The people who see their dreams come true are not the ones who avoid rejection; they are the ones who stay at the task despite the opposition. Rejection is coming, just like bad weather. The question is what you are going to do about it.

Alice Hixson, a salesperson, injected this piece of wisdom at a sales meeting: "If you look around the room, you will notice that the people who are the most successful are the ones who have received the most no's."

An insurance salesman keeps a record of how many calls he has to make in order to complete one sale. He talks to a certain number of people in order to sell one policy—that means many no's to collect one yes.

A state patrolman must live with a tremendous amount of rejection. Frequently his life is one of distributing speeding tickets to people who are furious. Seldom does he hear, "Officer, am I glad to see you!" If he didn't feel he was doing a higher good, his job would become nearly impossible.

Rejection isn't restricted to the business world. Think of the many parents and teenagers who stand back suspiciously eyeing each other. The young people are discarding their parents' control and life-style. At the same time the parents cannot accept the new ideas of the growing children. The result is enormous friction and conflict.

Divorcees are finding a type of rejection that they may not have imagined before. Someone has lived with him for two, five, or twenty years but no longer cares to. In essence he's saying, "I have gotten to know you well, even intimately, and I don't want you." It would be difficult not to take this personally.

Children often experience the same feelings. They may not be certain whether or not their parents want them. In fact, some know that their parents do *not* want them. Children under this type of deprivation may grow into adults who are overwhelmed with a sense of rejection.

The subject is both wide and deep. All of us suffer from the shock of rejection, and some of us are nearly paralyzed by its devastating effects.

Who can tell what we might do in life if we could get a good handle on controlling rejection? Not eliminating it—that's not a realistic goal or even a desirable one. But *getting control* over our reactions to rejection is a reasonable ambition.

There are mountains we could climb, new wonders we could create, talents we could set free, service we could perform, relationships we could develop. These and many more are possible once we have applied the following:

1. Accept being turned down as a normal part of life.
2. Find ways to get control over rejection.
3. Learn from each setback.
4. Bounce back.

Each of us has a wide reservoir of resilience. We get kicked around, but through some miracle of strength we manage to get up again. The mat is a place we visit, but we refuse to stay there.

A piece of sand is pushed into the oyster's world. That oyster completely and totally rejects the particle of sand. However, the sand holds on. Throughout the oyster's best efforts, it stubbornly refuses to budge. Eventually that grain of sand develops into a beautiful pearl. Its new value came as a result of being absolutely rejected.

This is not to say that we can turn every rejection into great worth or reverse each rejection to enthusiastic acceptance. Some situations will not and cannot be resolved. Your grouchy boss may be a cactus plant all his life, and God Himself will not change him. Your neighbor might give you an ugly stare no matter how many plates of cookies you send over.

In order to handle rejection we *must* begin by discarding our superman attitude. We cannot change everything. We cannot change everyone. Our superiority complex shows its pointed head. The truth is that many of us are upset because we cannot charm everyone. It is a fact we fail to accept. This inability serves as a dagger in our side. We will continue to be wounded, bleeding until we are healed by reality. Be the nicest person you can possibly be, but someone is still going to treat you like garbage.

We are not above rejection. Rejection is part of our lot.

Some rejection you deserve and some you do not. You can count on getting both kinds.

The book of Proverbs speaks bluntly: "A just man falls seven times and rises up again" (24:16 KJV).

Even the best of us gets dumped on. The difference is that not all of us get up again.

If Jesus Christ and God the Father can be rejected by human beings, we can hardly expect immunity.

Nelson Rockefeller's great ambition was to be President of the United States. He already had almost enormous wealth. His career included high office, but the Oval Office eluded Rockefeller because the body politic rejected him. No thanks! We don't want you! That's a terrible blow to the ego no matter what other assets you possess.

By now you must be convinced that you are a validated member of the human race. The rejection you face may be different, more frequent, and possibly more personal than that which other people encounter, but one fact is inescapable: As a person you will experience rejection. Shake hands with yourself: You are species rejectable!

The important question is what you are going to do about it. If you allow rejection to hold you hostage, you will lose the great experiences of life.

You will be held captive by the thought of being turned down.

A great deal of what appears to be laziness is in fact paralysis. We are afraid that if we do something, if we venture out, we are going to get our ego crushed. Therefore we hole up. Friends, relatives, and parents attribute it to a lack of ambition. In reality we can't stand the thought of being turned down.

Again, the Proverbs address this common feeling: "The slothful man says, 'There is a lion in the way; a lion is in the streets' " (26:13 KJV).

Who can argue with the logic? There *are* lions in the area. People *can* get hurt. The answer is not to lock yourself in, but to go out and become a lion-tamer. If you tame lions you can get injured, but you can also collect a magnificent array of beasts.

If you're like most individuals, you have a fair assortment of unfulfilled dreams. You would like to travel. You would like to go to graduate school. You would like to teach a class. You would like to get a better job. Unfortunately, if your present fear of rejection continues, those dreams will become like old paint cans. They have been opened but the paint was never used. Now it's dried up, cracked and useless. But if the brush had been applied at the right time, it could have produced some beautiful colors. Don't hold back the brush too long. And by all means don't close the lid on the jar. Paint! Paint! Paint!

Begin your beautiful picture by asking if your fears of rejection are based on reality or are merely phantoms. Are you afraid of ghosts that don't exist? If everyone who is afraid of rejection that isn't real would send me a dollar, I could retire in Tahiti.

Rich was sure that the manager of the clothing store did not like him. For years he avoided the store, believing he would be treated gruffly if he entered. Finally Rich attended a meeting where he was forced to shake hands with the store manager. To his total surprise the manager did not know him but was pleased to become acquainted!

Years of agony over nothing!

There is plenty of real, hard rejection going around. It is a shame to be belittled by phantom rejection.

Stories such as this are commonplace. We may suffer more from false rejection than we do from the real. What especially hurts is when brothers have not talked to brothers for decades because neither really understood, when separated couples remain parted because of mere rumors that the one did not care to see the other.

This is a particular problem among the thousands who would like to write. They have a story, an article, a book they want to see in print. However, the possibility of rejection is too high a wall for them to scale. The work they love remains in a lonely drawer. The people who could benefit by reading it are deprived—all because of a fear to try, not because they have been turned down but because they might be.

In families the ghost of false rejection can do even more damage. When young people and parents stop talking they begin to imagine more rejection than is actually there. For fear of being given the cold shoulder, they decide to take no risks. It's easier to stand back than take the chance that rejection might result.

The ghost has struck again.

A few simple guidelines could prevent the ghost from taking control.

Never believe you are rejected unless the person says so.

Too often we live in trembling fear over something we imagine. Despite our best attempts to read body languages and to pick up facial messages, we really aren't very good at it.

Most of the time we don't know if we have been rejected or are simply victims of the twitch.

A great many people we consider aloof and cold are in fact shy and hesitant. Often they would like to get to know you if only you would go further to break the ice. Do it!

After several discussions about forming a Christian support group, the individuals stopped meeting. Later they discovered that each person wanted the group to continue. However, each had felt the others wanted to disband. The ghost got them.

A simple disagreement is not the same as rejection.

Because someone doesn't want one thing you have does not mean that he does not want *you*. The person who rejects your ceramic may thoroughly enjoy you as a person.

It's common to confuse the two. We can't expect people to throw babies in the air over our every idea. To the contrary, often our better friends will be willing to tell us when we have a terrible project.

Fortunately, as many of us mature we learn to distinguish between professional rejection and personal rejection. If we do not learn, we do not survive well. After years of practice doctors often realize that to have their advice rejected does not mean that they are rejected. A hapless few never do learn it.

Maybe someone should have told the engineers of the Edsel. Possibly Wrong Way Corrigan needed a friend. Why didn't someone tell John Dillinger to get a job?

The disagreement over an idea is not the rejection of the person.

Promise yourself to try again.

For all you know, it may have been a bad day for the person who turned you down. You may have lost the opportunity on nothing more than bad liverwurst. Promise yourself that you will try again.

It's frequently the twelfth try that puts it in the bag. The first hug might be shrugged off, but the third one could become toasty warm.

Think about how many times you have been glad you went back. That's why some of us are married to the person we love.

Each of us has been kicked in the head at some time. We had our hopes high and thought we had the tiger by the tail. But just as we hit the crest someone dumped everything in on us.

Disgusted, angry, confused, we groveled in the dust wondering what happened. After a generous dose of self-pity we made our decision: We would get up; we would bounce back and grab the tiger again.

The story of hope is one about people who bounce back.

2

Types of Rejection

"Get out and never come back!"

That sounds unequivocal, and when you hear it you're left with few options. In most cases you would clear out and not return. After all, not many of us enjoy being barked at and treated like scum!

A famous musician, Roy Clark, said he was once told not to come back. Statements like that don't leave us average guys much to work with.

There are a few courageous souls who seem to prosper under that kind of dismissal, but not many. Such remarks are definite and final.

The problem is that most stories of rejection are not that clear. The word "no" is not as simple as it might appear. It might mean:

"No, not now."

"No, not that way."

"No, not that color."

"No, I don't feel well today."

"No, you are sewer scum."

"No! If I catch you in the yard again I'll sic the dog on you!"

Most men are hesitant to invite girls on dates because of two fears: They dread the thought of being told no, and they are petrified at the prospect of having to interpret that crisp reply.

A negative answer without an explanation drives the average male to the brink. A brief excuse helps a little. A definite conflict lessens the pressure. An invitation to ask her out again is a taste of heaven.

He needs to have a reason for being rejected. Ideally it has nothing to do with him personally.

How many of us have placed our hand on the phone, too petrified to dial the number? How often have we dialed all digits except the last? We can hear rejection coming like a train. We are afraid its steel wheels are about to crush our frame.

Girls play the same games. Why weren't they invited out to the big event? Was it because they were too tomboyish? Have they played too hard-to-get? Have they turned too many dates down? Some imagine they're so pretty that it inhibits the guys. Sometimes the girls blame the boys for being too dorky to invite them out.

If possible, they want to avoid the conclusion that they were personally rejected. Most often they're right.

It's hard to deal with rejection unless we accurately identify it. Taking wild and illusionary guesses makes the real problem impossible to cope with.

Parents frequently have difficulty solving problems with their children because they are fighting the wrong wars. Marriage partners drift apart when they fail to understand why they are drifting apart.

Most writers live with rejection. It wouldn't be uncommon for an aspiring author to literally be able to paper his walls with rejection slips. No matter how the cold slip or clever letter is worded, it's still hard not to take it personally. The writer has dared to express himself on paper; it is part of how he feels, what he thinks. In return he gets a piece of paper that says, "No. We don't want it. We are turning you down."

Because he is a professional, the writer tries hard to rise above it. He, like the dateless girl, tries to find reasons why he was not accepted. The writer looks for any encouraging word in the rejection: a complimentary phrase, a redeeming expression. He rationalizes that the publisher has too many manuscripts, that the company doesn't handle quality material. Finally, after playing mental gymnastics, he reaches the inevitable conclusion: "Everyone hates me."

A tax expert was giving advice to authors, and one sage comment was, "Be sure to save your rejection slips or else the IRS won't know you are a writer." He seemed to assume that most writers had nothing in print!

When it's difficult to distinguish between yourself and your project, it's hard to try again. It's rough to stand up and say, "Here I am—take another swing at me."

Many of us could bounce back if we knew what it was that knocked us down.

A mother makes a suggestion at the family table.

Immediately the ceiling caves in with objections. Daughter's eyes well up; son sinks in his chair and sulks; Dad puts his coffee cup down and reaches for the paper.

What happened? Do they hate her idea? Do they think she has an odd odor? Maybe neither is true. There could be other reasons why her idea was dead before it left her lips.

Begin with a careful analysis of the rejection. You may have to run it past a couple of friends to collect some objective opinions.

Knowing what knocked you down is the first step to *bouncing back*.

A quick checklist could be a great help. This is a sample. You might want to add to it.

Rejection of the object.

What you are selling or presenting could be genuine, certifiable trash.

Too often we have become blinded by our enthusiasm for our product.

While I was in college I sold portable radios from door to door. On hot nights in Washington, D.C., I would walk the streets with a radio playing loudly and talk to people as they sat on their front steps.

It was a neat, sharp little radio that you would think anyone would want. My biggest problem came from the fact that as I explained the great qualities of the modern miracle, the radio would stop playing as I spoke.

Naturally I skillfully smacked the set a couple of times as I described how easy it was to restart. Despite my swift handwork, the potential customer never looked the same again.

We have tremendous talents. We frequently use them to fool ourselves. Yet the product could be a real dud.

Have you ever tried to sell houseplants while aphids danced on your arm? Your product could be a real loser.

However, a couple of obstacles stop us from being objective.

1. Our need to make money.

2. Our love for a product we put together. It's possible that your hook rugs look awful and that your husband doesn't dare tell you.

Rejection of the situation.

Rest homes don't need pogo sticks!

Churches don't need gorillas!

Ladies' groups don't need wrenches!

Under most conditions that would seem obvious, but in this crazy world of "You can do anything," simple facts become obscured. There are a lot of dumb ideas running around, and you might have one by the leash. A gifted orator or slick writer has convinced you that you can do anything. Terrific. The only difficulty with that philosophy is that you can't.

If you believe you can do anything, you're heading for rejection. You definitely will take rejection personally. After all, you can do anything! Consequently, you go down the dumper without comprehending the real problem.

If all rejection is personal rejection, you're dead in the water. Check out the situation again.

A lady felt that the new church she was attending was cold to her ideas. No matter what she suggested, she couldn't get it adopted. How did she feel? What was her reaction? She was convinced they didn't like her. Defeated, she retreated to the back pew and wilted.

Unfortunately, the lady failed to see the real difference. The ideas which worked in her big-city church were inappropriate in the small town. She perished in the parish because she could not identify the real rejection.

Rejection of the presentation.

Maybe you didn't say it right!

Recently I presented a new idea to a committee. I knew it was something they would enjoy hearing about and be eager to participate in. As I presented the proposal I could see panic rise in their eyes. Instantly they were 100 percent against it.

I was so bewildered by their response that I immediately asked them to explain what I had said. From their explanation it was apparent that I had presented it incorrectly. They didn't hear what I said because of the way I said it.

It happens all the time: Inaccurate words. Improper description. Inappropriate challenge. Disastrous results.

Allen got blown out of the saddle at a committee meeting. After a couple of hours of depression he began to scrutinize his presentation. He knew the idea was as good as gold, and he knew this was the right situation. Allen soon concluded that he had shocked the committee. He had failed to do his groundwork. He had handed them the idea abruptly, like a full-grown tree, but he had failed to prepare the ground correctly.

If he had dropped some hints prior to the presentation . . . if he had discussed the concept with a few individuals . . . if he had briefly introduced the subject several months before—it might have been accepted.

But the shock was too much. They rejected the idea as a defense mechanism, as one shakes off cold water when it's thrown in his face.

Fortunately, he shrugged off the simplistic answer. He did not merely declare himself deficient and run his finger through the electric can opener.

Rejection of themselves.

It's possible that you lost the day because of bad ham. We will never know how often we have been turned down because the individual had a lousy lunch.

You hit your husband with an idea just as he comes in the door. He reacts, "All you know how to do is spend money!" In the early-morning rush you ask your wife if there are any clean socks and she snaps, "Everybody wants something. What am I, a slave?"

That person isn't turning down you or your idea. His creative system has collapsed. You may be transmitting beautifully, but his receiver is cracked.

Sometimes the human element is easy to detect. The person we are talking to is crisp, impatient, rude, even hostile. If he's not normally that way, perhaps his digestive system has rung his bell. Maybe he has just received news that "60 Minutes" wants to interview him. It's what we used to call "being off your feed."

We can't remove human feelings, nor do we want to. However, we need to accept them for what they are and try again. Anyone knocked out by hot dogs and relish needs to bounce back. Another trip to the same person could result in one fantastic victory.

The first time Charlie and I met, he chewed me out for walking on a floor he had just waxed. Boy, was he a grouch! If he wanted people to stay off the floor he should have put up a sign or a rope.

I don't know which one of us had bad bananas for lunch, but I'm glad we tried meeting each other again. We remained friends for 25 years.

Make a mental note: If the person you want to reach is having a bad day, he isn't rejecting you. Be sure to make that call again later.

Rejection of the person.

Now for the bad news! All of us are rejected sometimes merely because of our person.

We saved this fact for last because we wanted to let you down gently. Sometimes we get turned down because of our hair, our smile, our beard, our build, our gender, our clothing, our sense of humor, or a long list of intangibles.

Yes, Virginia, people do get personally rejected. It isn't all a fairy tale.

One lady was kept off all church committees because she was demanding, dictatorial, and generally obnoxious. Cruel words, but it does happen.

A woman visited our house selling a well-known product. To this day I don't know if the stuff worked. But I do know that she grated us so badly that we probably wouldn't have bought a boat from her in a flood.

There aren't many really revolting people, though there are some. However, most of us prove aggravating to someone. We are the wrong mix.

He may be the salesman of the year to his company, but he will always be a headache to you. She may be Lady of the Year in Oregon, but she is a migraine in your house. She may be Mother Teresa's best friend, but she gives you heartburn.

Those are the realities of life. And as long as we wear this crusty shell it will continue to be true. Mr. Rogers may not want you in his neighborhood. Personal rejection is real.

However, generally the problem is that we are *too willing* to accept this fact. We think each rejection is a rejection of us personally. If the television repairman doesn't come on time, we assume he hates us. (He probably doesn't even know us.) When we don't get mail, we imagine that the Book of the Month Club is trying to deprive us of a special novel.

It would be far more helpful to try to investigate the real reasons for rejection. Any of the ones we have listed are possible, plus several more.

Do not automatically accept personal rejection as the culprit. Many of us have suffered enormous loss because we did not really understand why we were rejected.

The crucial question to ask after a rejection is, "Do I want to go back and try again, or would I rather forget it?" In order to answer that, you must try to decide what kind of rejection you face.

Many rejections are reversible!

Read that again.

Not *every* rejection is reversible—that's arguing perfection. People who believe they can do anything should try swallowing a Studebaker.

Nevertheless, many rejections are temporary. If you determine what caused the rejection, you may be able to make adjustments and try again.

Most successful people are old buddies with rejection. They have met it often and learned to deal with it. Happily married couples have encountered rejection in their own homes and bounced back.

Generally people will not reject you as a person. Over 90 percent of the people you meet will treat you with kindness and respect. That's the way they want to be treated, and they are eager to dispense the same medicine. Even those who are uncomfortable with you will dismiss you with a reasonable amount of civility.

After you narrow down the cause of the rejection, ask yourself if the problem can be corrected. Can you give a better presentation? Can you appeal to their situation? Can you choose an hour when the person in charge will have a docile stomach?

If you can make alterations, by all means go back. Go back. Go back. Most stories of victory are stories of people who went back. The successful stories of those who refused to go back are as scarce as golden coconuts.

A school principal said that student teachers come to him and say they want another teacher. They give a wide array of complaints. The class is unruly, the teacher is intolerant or picky, and so on.

The principal listens to all the reasons why the two are incompatible. Then he looks at the college student and says, "Go back." Go back and adjust. Go back and learn. Go back and conquer yourself. If you run from people you have difficulty with, you will run forever. Go back!

That's tough advice because it's hard to do. But those who go back are usually the ones who have done the jobs, have gotten the accounts, have changed the committee, have revitalized the church, have kept their families, and have won the Hamilton County cookie-baking contest.

3

The Fear
of Success

Years ago a high school principal asked for the title of my address to the graduating class. The exact wording has long been lost, but it included the word "success." When the principal heard the word, he nearly went blind with fury.

He insisted the word was a curse and the concept was pagan. All of that and he hadn't even heard the speech!

Learning to operate a camera is a success. Feeding the poor is a success story. You can be successful at reading a book. The love your family has for each other is about as successful as a person can get.

To succeed is to set a goal and meet it. If along the way you need to alter the goal, you also alter your success.

With this definition there is no doubt that God wants you to succeed. He wants you to dream and see those dreams come true. Maybe your dream is to build a bird feeder and care for some of His

31

creatures. Success may be no more complicated than that.

Throw off the ugly concepts. You might not become a millionaire in 90 days. God doesn't owe you a yacht or a limousine.

It would be interesting to know how many people fail because they are afraid to succeed. There seems to be more fear of success than we might realize.

Normally we think people do not try because they are afraid of failure and rejection. There is no doubt about it: We don't enjoy looking like fools. Most of us are reluctant to advertise our inabilities. We don't enter spelling bees if we can't spell.

However, there may be a significantly large number of us who are just as frightened of succeeding.

An artist was evaluating his approach to creativity and concluded that he used it to avoid success. He prided himself in his ability to paint obscure, noncommercial subjects. However, it also caused him to wonder if his need to paint obscure subjects was not caused by his secret desire to remain obscure. After all, if his paintings sold, they would become open to criticism. Subconsciously he may have been trying to escape anguish by sidestepping success.

What happens if we're successful?

More will be expected of us.

Success brings responsibility. If you become chairman of the committee, you will have to preside. The responsibility will take time. The buck will stop at your telephone. Maybe it would be better to avoid the demands of success.

If you've seen a stress chart, you know how painful success can be. Smack in the middle of the list is "outstanding personal achievement." Success becomes a burden to most of us. Progress becomes an emotional shock producing a high level of anxiety. Many of us work hard to avoid the stress of success.

More people will criticize us.

Success has a hydraulic effect. It lifts you up and you become an easy target for potshots.

A large number of people would like to write. However, they realize that if something is published, people will read it. They then fear that those who read it will think it is poor. This is an extremely common problem. Consequently, they write material and do not send it for fear it will be accepted. Success can hurt.

We must leave the comfort of the couch of failure.

Despite our ardent protests to the contrary, many of us like to fail. We're used to it. It's like an old hat, a pair of worn slippers, a favorite rocking chair.

That's why many of us do not like to change anything in our house. Change will call itself to people's attention. Attention is risky since it also invites disapproval. Therefore by refusing to innovate we retreat to the old method. And we retreat willingly. We retreat joyfully. There's no sense in getting our feelings hurt.

When we speak of success we aren't talking of business alone. We include the entire gamut of personal relationships, personal fulfillment, family interaction, church involvement, and more. Some of us choose to fail in a number of areas. A few of us prefer to fail in all.

Knowledge is responsibility. So is success.

Consider the person who votes against every improvement. He wants things to get better. He has probably stated it many times. But at the same time he is afraid of success.

What if they do vote it in? Then they will have to try it. If they try it, it might work. And if it works, the ceiling of protests might fall in.

Success invites attack.

The tragedy is that a man wants change. He longs for a better way. He's tired of the boring routine of the old. And yet he's torn by the bitter reality of success. Success might cause pain and discomfort. In the final call he votes against it.

What of the woman whose business is placing book racks? If she goes into a store and asks for permission to place a rack, she runs a risk. The manager might say yes. If he says yes, she has all kinds of problems.

Success in this case means that the books have to sell or she could fail. It means that she must now enter into a relationship of discussion with the manager. She will also inherit the responsibility of keeping the rack stocked on a regular basis.

All of this because it worked. If she had failed, none of this would have happened.

The young man who asks a girl to marry him faces the same contradiction. If she refuses him, he will be crushed. If she says yes he could be overwhelmed. No wonder many couples are perplexed at the wedding!

What if something doesn't work? Indeed, what if it does?

No doubt you have noticed that only those fall who first have risen. Only that which goes up can come down. The higher we go, the greater distance we can tumble. With that principle in the back of our minds, we would just as soon stay where we are.

This is part of what many of us weigh before we buy a house. We are reluctant to purchase one that is too fancy lest we be designated as ostentatious. If we look too good we could invite the disapproval of friends and acquaintances. Not eager to invite criticism, we aim for a more modest dwelling.

The fear of success results in widespread anxiety and even guilt. On the one hand we admire the American spirit. It is purported to be adventurous, innovative, and courageous. We would like to strike out and accomplish the daring.

Yet we are held in check by the embarrassment of success. How will we justify our accomplishments? How can we explain breaking from the pack?

The fact is that God wants to be good to us. His goodness is not based on our loveliness; rather, it originates from God's nature. He wants to be generous because He is generous by nature.

This is why Jesus could promise us that when we ask our Father for good things He does not hand us dust. God likes to see happiness come into our lives (Matthew 7:7-11).

Often students drown in this dilemma. They feel the pressure to succeed in school. Many would enjoy doing well. However, good grades summon two curses. First, peer pressure prevents them from breaking from the pack and becoming outstanding students. Second, responsibility frequently accompanies good work. If they succeed, much will be required. Should they fail, teachers tend to be happy with crumbs.

Success means stress. Having visited it, many decide to opt for mediocrity.

One student did well in speech class but soon found the pressure undesirable. With each speech the teacher demanded greater excellence. The student soon noticed that those who did poorly received accolades for any flimsy presentation. This student soon decided to join the happier stragglers.

In the past the feeling has been prevalent among many women. They have feared success lest they would be less desirable to men. Pity the poor female who could defeat men at golf or tennis! Woe on the woman who was too sharp in the business world!

In one office two women worked for years in the accounting department. As each new head of the department assumed his post, the women would teach him his job. Yet, as women, they could never be considered for the post. Women were not supposed to be too successful. If they did, they often lost their status.

The fear of good fortune continues to plague much of the population. It's expressed in the mountain-valley syndrome. This bit of conventional wisdom tells us that after every mountaintop experience we can expect a valley to follow.

On the surface this sounds reasonable. Life is a series of ups and downs. However, under closer scrutiny it becomes a curse. We fear the good times because they bring on the bad ones. Therefore we shy away from too many mountains. Happiness will be followed by sadness, so we had better avoid too much happiness. We would be wise to maintain a low-key life. It is as if we must pay for our ups with downs.

There's no denying that life has plenty of pitfalls. But the trap is to believe they are links in a chain. Why can't we have five or six good experiences in a row before we have one bad one? Surely we have had enough times when four or five bad times have grouped together!

The fact is that our successes far outweigh our failures. Most of the time we are successful.

A high school girl explained her fear of succeeding in terms of ridicule. She wanted to try out for cheerleader. Her fear was not that she would fail to make it; her biggest reluctance came from the possibility that she would succeed.

She was convinced that if she made it people would say, "Who does she think she is? Why, she can't even jump! They must have been desperate for cheerleaders." Winning the position would be worse than losing it.

Her list of priorities ran in reverse order: The very best thing she could do would be to not try out for cheerleader. The second best thing she could do would be to try out for it and be rejected. The worst thing she could do would be to try out and be accepted.

She decided not to try out.

To try for it precluded some type of rejection.

To avoid rejection, she chose to do nothing.

How much of this contorted logic finds its origin in our theology? Do we think that God does not believe we deserve to be happy and that consequently He does not want us happy? Most of the concepts we hold have a direct bearing on how we see God. If God is simply tolerating us, we tend to have a low view of ourselves. However, if God is pleased to have us around, if He is happy to see us happy, our outlook becomes vastly improved.

Imagine for a moment that God is absolutely thrilled with you. You may have to read that sentence again. You might even want to get a glass of water.

Suppose God is not performance-centered. What if He loves me for who I am instead of for what I do? What if He loves me when I am good and when I am bad?

Love is not a historical event: God did not love me simply on the cross; *He actively loves me now.* Often Christian love becomes a grim business: "God loves you, so you'd better watch out."

But suppose God loves us and would like to see us happy. That's what love normally wants (1 Corinthians 13:4-7). Then God doesn't stand around waiting to zap us. Instead, He becomes our best backer. He would like to see us succeed on whatever level we are functioning.

Some students are reluctant to volunteer answers in class because it becomes embarrassing. They are several strides ahead of the others in knowledge of the subject but are afraid to admit it. If they raise their hand too much, other students become disgruntled. They had better retreat back into the pack before becoming disdained as a know-it-all.

When you have teenagers you have conflict. Yet conflict doesn't cause you to stop loving them. You still want what's best for them. Sometimes you discipline them, possibly even with stern measures. But you remain their number one cheerleader.

Try to see God in the same light. His best teaching is not punishment. His attitude is not negative. God fully appreciates the value of expressing love in open-armed acceptance. He believes in positive reinforcement.

That doesn't negate the call to sacrifice. It doesn't belittle the need to give of yourself. We aren't released of our responsibilities. But it does guarantee us an everlasting, consistent love.

God is thrilled with you. He would like to change you. He wishes you would sit up, not gulp your food, go to bed a little earlier, and cut down on fatty foods. But He's still thrilled with you and loves to see you happy.

"Happy are those who long to be just and good, for they shall be completely satisfied.

Happy are the kind and merciful, for they shall be shown mercy.

Happy are those whose hearts are pure, for they shall see God.

Happy are those who strive for peace—they shall be called the sons of God.

Happy are those who are persecuted because they are good, for the Kingdom of Heaven is theirs" (Matthew 5:6-10 TLB).

God seems to have a special concern for our well-being. That's why His Son gave us formulas for happiness.

4

The Need
to Be Perfect

When I met her she didn't have a hair out of place. Her dress was impeccable. Each word was measured. Immediately you got the feeling that she couldn't let go. Every action was guarded. She felt the need to be faultless, and that compulsion kept her as tightly wound as a spring.

It was a shame, because she obviously was a pleasant person. She would have been fascinating to get to know, but there was no way the woman would let go.

Perfectionism is a cruel tyrant: You can't please it and you can't escape its reach. In the long run the drive for perfection will hurt you instead of lifting you up to higher goals.

Studies indicate that people who are not perfectionists usually accomplish more than those who are. Most of the time those who can relax and go with the punches make more income and rise higher on the occupational ladder. Perfectionists tend to earn thousands of dollars less

41

than their laid-back counterparts.

Money is only a small part of the problem. Perfectionists are likely to dream less, take fewer risks, experience poorer health, have weaker family relationships, and generally find life a big pain.

Perfectionists are hard to identify. All of them would argue that they are not perfect. However, that's only a superficial agreement. Internally they feel a relentless drive to do everything beyond criticism. They would be willing to say that they make mistakes—of course, everyone does. But woe to the poor fool who specifically names a mistake they created! The perfectionist will fight to prove he made no mistake, and, unable to accomplish that, will later collapse in total despair. To come apart in front of other people is definitely forbidden, so he will cry alone.

To clarify our terms, let's ask what we mean by perfectionism. "Doing a good job" does not define perfectionism. Everyone should want to do a good job. That leads to satisfaction and a feeling of accomplishment. A good job makes it possible for you to live with your fellow workers, yourself, and God.

However, pushing one step further and trying to do everything beyond possible reproach explains perfectionism. This borders on the brink of madness.

If you strive for perfection you must eliminate activities at which you do not excel. Since you can't do everything correctly, you soon learn to try only the things at which you are superior. If you discover that you don't swing a bat well, you give up swinging bats. Should you lose at tennis, you give up tennis. Before long you have developed a narrow alley. That alley is lined with things you do well. Since you can't risk defeat, nothing else is permitted to enter your life.

Perfectionists must become masters of control. They refuse to be swept away in a moment of frivolous excitement.

Usually people think they are motivated by excellence. In fact many are driven by fear.

The cruel tyrant perfectionism will not be appeased. There is no end to the sacrifices that must be made at his altar. After you complete one deed as perfectly as possible, the next task waits for renewed perfection. Vacations must be precise. Clothing must match the occasion exactly. Children must excel. Even the dog may not be a mutt.

Does it all sound miserable? It is.

Why do people do it? Some of us don't know any better. We think it is the only way to travel. Others are afraid of the alternatives. If we let go and do something less than perfect, what are the consequences? We aren't sure. We may be out of control, and we can't afford that risk.

Many of us know people who are split-perfectionists. At work they're flawless, but when they come home they unfold and become sloppy. Some are living on the edge at work: They are living a perfectionism that they can barely support. The tension of pushing as hard as possible at the job leaves them with no energy at home. In effect they cannot pretend at both places, and consequently they resort to extremes.

The need to be perfect often takes its toll on

professionals. Doctors, lawyers, dentists, and psychiatrists who feel they can't make mistakes may be living under an impossible strain. When they find the shield of perfection too heavy to hold, they frequently drop it with disastrous results. Exhausted from trying, some attempt to end their own lives.

This curse hurts not only adults but also our children, as we pass it down. This accounts for some of the self-destruction we find among young people.

Consider the parent who continues to negatively react to his child's accomplishments. A mother recently told me she failed her son. The boy proudly showed her his report card displaying all B's and one C. Her response was "That's terrific. Now next time we can get that C up to a B."

She tried to tell him the report card was good, but actually she said it was not. "Why did I do that?" she asked. "It was the right time to praise him, but instead I made sure I got a dig in."

Some children can't win. If they come close to meeting the standard, we automatically raise it. We try to justify ourselves by saying we only want them to do their best. The carrot keeps moving. Our real goal is perfection, and the child must bear the burden.

The great American dream has always been that our children should do better than we did. That's a lot to ask. Many families have a home, two cars, and a dog. Dad and Mom each have a master's degree or better. On vacation the family goes skiing or wears leis on sandy beaches.

Our children are expected to do better than this? Some will, but many will not. Yet they live under the pressure of their parents' expectation. Couple this with society's expectations, then add television's idealism, and young people drown in perfectionism.

The result is frustrated, burned out, sometimes suicidal young people.

Much of this pressure could be defused if parents would back down. We will discuss this more completely in our chapter on Preparing Children for Acceptance.

If the chains of perfectionism are heavy and confining, what can we do to break them? People are too complicated for simple solutions, but the following are suggestions that may help. For those who implement them, life-changing results may follow.

Today I will make peace with myself.

The perfectionist is at war. He knows he isn't perfect and can't be. What he *knows* and what he *does* are at war with each other.

Call a truce. Go directly to peace negotiations. Tell yourself you will no longer expect yourself to be perfect.

What a relief! You will no longer need to waste your energy trying to do the impossible. There is no reason to try to impress yourself.

From now on you can tell your children, "I don't know." You can tell your neighbor, "I can't afford it." You can tell your wife, "I misplaced it." You can tell your boss, "I forgot to do it."

Today you're free to play Ping-Pong with the guy who always beats you. You know the fun of playing. You get a few good shots in and your backhand has one amazing return. It's fun to merely be there having a good time.

Today I will accept my faults.

It may sound old hat to some people, but we are sinners—not in the general sense but in the specific sense. We do things that are wrong. Perfectionism is a denial of that reality. It's the dream of rising above imperfections.

Not long ago I insulted a woman. If I had a brain in my head, I would not have said such a stupid thing. But I did. Afterward I went into the pits. How could I do that? That was terrible. I can't do anything right.

A moment's failure was quickly translated into total failure. The fine balance is to realize that I do things that are wrong, but that doesn't mean I am totally wrong.

It's part of the internal war. Part of me cannot tolerate any mistakes. That part must learn to accept my imperfections.

We have the mistaken idea that other people do not have faults. Others are dressed neat as gnats, career moving ahead, always saying the right things, and we imagine they have it all together. If they have it all together and we don't, there is obviously something wrong with us.

Our logic is wrong: They are not perfect. When we accept the fact that they have faults, we can better accept our own. After all, we are all sinners (Romans 3:10,23). That covers all of us very snugly!

Today I will enjoy a half-loaf.

The half-loaf approach to life has its values. In simple terms it means that you can't do everything but you'll do what you can. You will be content to go home at quitting time. You will take time to chat with other people. You will still do work that you can be proud of, but you will not demand perfection of yourself.

If we take this approach, some things will be left undone. Some things *should* be left undone.

Those who cannot live with a half-loaf are extremely demanding on their fellow workers, on themselves, and often on their families. They have more burnout, more alcoholism, more absenteeism, more turnover, more sickness, more friction, and in the long run less productivity.

A man who adopted this approach expressed it well: "I figured I have 30 years of work to do. I can do it in 15 years and die early or I can stretch it out over 40 years and appreciate life."

The perfectionist has trouble combing beaches. He has trouble watching loons on the pond. He has trouble playing with two-year-olds on the floor.

Today I will forgive myself.

Each of us needs to issue a full pardon to ourselves—a pardon that covers both our past mistakes and our future ones. That looks good on paper, but most of us have difficulty carrying this out. None of us could live with an unforgiving God, and yet many of us have become that rigid toward ourselves.

Some of us continuously castigate ourselves for not getting the degree we had dreamed of. We blame our problems on that failure. It serves as a handicap which we drag around to remind ourselves of our inadequacies.

Why does it bother us so badly? Is it because we

believe we could have been perfect? Because we *should* have been perfect? We imagine that perfection was within our grasp and we failed ourselves.

If we wanted that degree, then naturally we should have had it. That's perfectionism. Since we did not get it, we see vulnerability. Vulnerability is something we cannot tolerate.

The result of this faulty reasoning is 10 years of flogging yourself. For some it's 20 or 30 years. We are beating ourselves for not being perfect.

Isn't it time to release the prisoner? To tell him it's all right? To offer him the simple grace of forgiveness?

The first step to forgiveness is to accept the fact that we are not perfect and cannot be. The second step is to stop trying to be perfect.

The people easiest to make feel guilty are parents. Parents rehearse their mistakes for years. They pay emotionally, physically, and financially for the errors they think they have committed.

It's true that they weren't perfect, but they weren't supposed to be perfect. They *couldn't* be perfect. Far better if they could accept the things they did beautifully, and forgive themselves for their mistakes! Not only will *they* be better off, but so will their children.

The forgiveness of God and the forgiveness of our friends is of limited value. Read that again. We cannot experience real release until we forgive ourselves.

Today I will relax with God.

God isn't mad at you! That will come as a big disappointment to people who have run their lives on the premise that God is upset. That belief will turn them into introspective perfectionists. Drop the idea! It's bad theology. It's a terrible concept of God.

Some people have presented God as being half-angry most of the time. They have reduced Him to purely human terms. He comes across as moody, unhappy, and generally dispirited. To some people God looks like a sour character on a Tums commercial.

Recently I asked a group how many of them would like to have God around as a personal friend. Most of the heads shook no immediately.

What kind of a God have we created? He sounds more like a steaming and rocking pressure cooker than He does Deity!

Jesus Christ stressed a relationship of friendliness. He called his followers into close and sharing partnership (John 15:14). Even tough doubters like Thomas were handled with patience and not harshness (John 20:27).

At one point in my life I decided to relax with God. I hadn't been a Christian long. But during that short period it seemed like I heard at least half a million do's and don't's. Every minister, teacher, and back-pew philosopher told me what to do. Doubtless they meant well. They wanted to make me perfect.

According to them God wanted me to be a missionary, a teacher, and a personal evangelist—and to attend every service any committee ever devised! People didn't hint at this. They said it directly.

I'll never forget one minister saying, "If you love God you'll be here." You can bet I was there. The list of things God wanted from me was endless.

One day sitting in a pew waiting for another barrage of instructions, I knew I had had it. Frustrated, I told God, "Please take me as I am or why don't we just forget it?" I knew I couldn't be a Christian if I had to be perfect.

From that day on I never again saw God as the Great Grouch in the Sky. I can relax with God. He loves me exactly as I am. There's no doubt He would like to see me clean up my act, but He isn't breathing smoke out of His nostrils.

Another minister used to say, "If you miss the perfect will of God, He will put you on the shelf." I must have heard him say that 30 times. I could picture myself crunched up and stuffed on a high shelf someplace.

Relax with God. He knows we aren't perfect. Why don't we know it too?

The Bible uses the word "perfect," but not in the same sense we kick around. People don't become perfect.

Too many young people have given up the Christian life because they felt they couldn't make God happy. Someone should have told them that God isn't mad at them. Relax!

Generally speaking, perfectionists are performance-oriented. They believe their value is dependent on what they do. What gives them worth? It's their ability to advance, to sell, to promote, to arrange, to entertain, to accomplish. Consequently, if these were to cease, the person would feel worthless.

We need to be aware of the dangers of that outlook.

To begin with perfectionism is elitist. Fundamentally it says that some people are more valuable than others. One surgeon is worth 10 street cleaners. One corporation president is worth 25 policemen. If we conclude that what the corporation president does is more important than what the policeman does, we conclude that the person himself is more important.

I have a friend who works at the city dump. He had excellent grades in school, sings exceptionally well, and enjoys books. However, he didn't choose to go the traditional route of success. Many people are dumbfounded at this. They consider his life a great waste. He is less valuable in their eyes because of what he does.

By that standard, A students are more important than D students. They warrant extra time, patience, and guidance.

Recently I attended a seminar and asked a woman what she did. She responded by saying that this was what everyone was asking her. She said she now realized that who you are depends on what you do.

This makes the average, warm human being of minimal value. Only the productive achiever is considered worthwhile. The man who works at the local lumberyard, fishes on Fridays, and loves his family gets low marks in this system.

The ultimate conclusion of perfectionism is disastrous: What happens when you can no longer perform? Those who cannot produce are placed in the back row to wait for old age to consume them.

As Doug Bildt pointed out, God loves the imperfect. Otherwise He would have eliminated Adam and Eve and started over. Instead, He took the sinful and chose to keep loving them.

Not every perfectionist sits on the board of a large corporation. Not all are hard drivers bound for success. Many perfectionists live in failure, their demise cursed by perfectionism.

They have become paralyzed by the fear of being less than perfect. Afraid they will not play a trumpet perfectly, they refuse to play at all. Unable to take a novice status, they will not learn to ski. Convinced they can never be the company's top salesman, they reject the job entirely.

These are nonfunctioning perfectionists. Because their standards are so high, there is no way they can compete with themselves. Defeated before they start, they drop back and idle their motor.

Perfectionism is rejecting ourselves. We serve an illusion—a ghost that knows nothing of reality. If we chase that illusion, we will miss the pleasure of knowing the real us.

The need to appear perfect has led to many heartaches in Christian families. We don't discuss conflicts we have with our teenagers because we believe we aren't supposed to have conflicts. Because they aren't discussed in classes, groups, or counseling, difficulties are allowed to continue to grow. The facade of perfection is of greater importance to us than finding solutions to problems.

Idealism is another aspect of perfectionism. We set a perfect standard and imagine that this ideal is attainable. Since we cannot reach the ideal, it becomes important to at least *appear* faultless. This need to pretend results in enormous pressure, and eventually that pressure causes eruptions.

For many people the day of freedom will come. They will be able to let their hair down, walk barefoot in the park, and admit that they enjoy George Jones records. They will be free to be fat, free to read only half a book, free to say they have some real questions about God, free to wear green socks. Not free to be obnoxious, but free to be themselves.

Then they will dance on top of the grave of perfectionism!

5

Short Pain, Long Pain

Have you ever tried to avoid going to the dentist? I have many times. What did I expect to gain? If I waited long enough, would the tooth heal? Maybe the industry would invent a miracle spray and they could coat enamel over my problem area!

Hoping against reality, I imagined I could get a better deal later. Somehow there would be less pain, less discomfort if I could put it off another week. Maybe I would even die. To die with untended teeth would be to rob life of its pain!

Almost none of this reasoning has any substance in truth. If I want to escape pain, my best bet is to handle it now. Today. The alternative is to live uneasily for weeks or months, dreading the unknown and adding to my suffering. In the final confrontation I will probably face more agony when I am forced to face the dentist.

Given the option to accept short pain now or long pain over a period of time, most of us elect the long route.

That's right—we choose long pain.

John was involved in a fair-paying job when he was offered a better one. It was precisely what John wanted, but he wondered how to quit his present job. The thought of it kept him awake.

How could he tell his boss he was going to leave? Who would replace him? How much notice should he give? Weeks turned into months as John found himself immobile.

John was accepting long, excruciating suffering because he wanted to dodge the pain. It couldn't be done.

We need to give our decisions due consideration, and we need to take time to plan a civil way to deliver the news, but we *don't* need to make the problem worse by putting things off.

If we choose a long-pain approach to life we live with much pain. We accept it as a way of life.

We vote for long pain almost daily. Saying yes can be an attempt to duck short-term pain: We don't want people mad at us. We bake cookies, wash cars, feed their tiger, clean out their snake pit, grab their electrical wires, eat chicken feathers, and let their child eat our shoe. Anything as long as we don't say no.

Many times we want to say yes. However, "yes" and "no" should become roses, each handed out carefully.

"I decided to get a job and I'm a lot happier," Linda told us. "When I was a housewife, every organization in town called me to bake, rake, sew, or clean. I could never say no. At least with a job I get paid."

Did Linda escape from a home she loved because she couldn't say no? Did she vote for long pain because she couldn't wrestle with short pain?

The next time you hang up the phone after saying yes when you meant no, take a short inventory of yourself. How does it make you feel to say the opposite of what you meant?

How do you feel about yourself?

Do you feel like seaweed because you couldn't do what you really wanted to? Are you being tossed around, a victim of whatever the sea wants to do with you?

It's a degrading experience. You know you weren't strong enough to say what you meant. You sense the fact that something is seriously wrong. Yet you know you'll probably say yes the next time too.

How do you feel about your real responsibilities?

Will they suffer because you've stretched further than you should have? What strain might be placed on your family and friends?

Frequently we cause pain for other people because we can't control our own boundaries. Stress, guilt, overwork, and frustration each place an added weight on those close to us.

How do you now feel about the person who called you?

We tend to be Jekyll and Hyde on this one. Often the phone conversation sounds pleasant, cooperative, and even appreciative. However, when we hang up, our face turns ashen and our tone hostile. Why does that butterbrain always call? He could have taken care of it without dragging me in!

It isn't fair to the person who asked. Some are callous and insist that you help no matter how you feel. But others would never want you to do it if you had serious conflicts. Some charming people are being called terrible names merely because we lack the courage to offer a polite no.

How do you feel about your dreams?

We each have a list of things we're waiting to do. Those creative dreams must be left on the back burner because we allow ourselves to be imprisoned. We are locked in by our refusal to say no. It's a prison we accepted with a smile in our voice and frustration in our heart.

How do you feel about the cause you accepted?

The job you have begrudgingly agreed to may be a first-rate enterprise. It might be encased in nobleness. But because you feel trapped, your opinion of this project will probably become much lower. Your spirit as a worker may be reserved. Possibly the project will suffer because it has collected an assortment of workers who do not really care to be there.

All because we can't say no.

We choose long pain instead of short pain.

We spread pain on family, friends, and workers because we hope to elude a bit of pain.

When I pastored a country church in Kansas, we lived across the road in the parsonage—two buildings standing alone in the middle of beautiful wheatfields and pastures.

Once a month the Ladies' Aid Society met at the church. A dozen or so cars formed a half-circle in the parking lot directly across from where we lived.

After we had pastored there for a year my wife, Pat, told me calmly that she no longer planned to attend the Ladies' Aid Society. There wasn't anything wrong with it, she explained, but it wasn't her bag.

My first reaction was that we would soon have to be moving! Surely no church could tolerate having their pastor's wife drop out of such a sacred institution.

My second reaction was deep pride. Pat wanted to be her own person. Why should she have to belong to a group simply to protect my job? Pat never attended again.

To the credit of the church members, no one ever said a word of complaint to us. We don't know what they thought, but they never said a word.

Caving in with a yes is based on the premise that negatives cause more trouble than positives. It's the hope that peace can be maintained by agreeing to do things that we don't want to do.

Sometimes that's true. All of us agree to take the long pain at times, and we should. People do things for us that they don't want to do, and we should for them.

We also know that it gets out of hand. The real goal is to control yes and no, not simply to turn to all no's.

Control is the key.

If we lose control, we may turn to all no's. Frustrated, we decide we can't handle decisions. We build a brick wall of defense and turn everything down. In doing this we victimize ourselves. We miss many good opportunities to help other people because we can't trust our ability to reply.

Dropping out is one of the extreme results of not being able to control our reactions.

Another extreme example is found in unhappy marriages. It's amazing how many couples married because one of them couldn't say no. The person wanted to say no, meant no, and may have said no several times. Unfortunately, she (or he) ended up married to someone she wanted to turn down.

Unable to handle short pain, she bought years of pain. Maybe decades. Maybe half a century.

This kind of marriage isn't as infrequent as some might guess.

Many adults endure years of pain because they can't resist demanding parents. One couple went to his parents' home once a week without fail. His mother was in poor health, and anytime he hinted that they might not visit, she began to relapse.

It was tearing his family apart. His wife felt strangled by the weekly trek and the children were distraught. Total turmoil existed because he couldn't take the risk of a negative.

Not everyone who says yes is a sucker. Many people are doing volunteer work with the greatest of joy and dedication. They're to be admired and encouraged. Not everyone who is kind to his parents is a fool. They're to be congratulated.

The problem is *entrapment*. Too many people are boxed in where they don't want to be, boxed in where they *should not* be.

They need to find freedom. Otherwise the widespread damage may be great.

If we can get a reasonable handle on how to

respond, there are many healthy benefits. They will allow you to lead a fuller and more confident life.

There are some things that will probably happen if you vote for short pain by taking control.

1. *You gain respect.*

If you exercise self-control, self-respect is almost always an immediate reward. When you practice self-control, other people are far more willing to grant you respect—a double benefit.

Amazingly, we refuse to say no because we believe the exact opposite. We're afraid we will have trouble living with ourselves and with others if we say no.

Those who respect us are willing to accept a kind refusal. Often people are shocked when you say yes. Hardly anyone in their organization thought you would go along with it. Someone said, "Let's give a call and see what he says."

If you had said no, they may have understood far more easily. They may be pleased you agreed to do it, but they may also be mystified.

A lady called to ask me if I could speak to her group. I didn't want to speak but couldn't say no. After sputtering around I finally squeaked out a feeble "I don't think so this time." Calmly she replied, "That's all right. A lot of members wanted Ed Brown. I think I'll call him."

Big deal. Me and my Messiah complex! If I turn it down they'll get someone else.

Often the person asking understands. We're the ones who become afraid that they will think ill of us.

2. *You gain personality.*

We may be in danger of becoming someone we

never wanted to be. Our personalities are flexible and often shift. Financial hardship has a way of altering our dispositions. Falling in love tends to make us lilted and pleasant. Excessive pressure can restrict us and cause us to withdraw.

If we take a victim position and feel compelled to do what others want, our personality can take a beating. Others are shaping us. They tell us where to be when. They also supply the whys and hows. Because we are unable to find the handle and become who we want to be, others are free to form us.

The freedom of choice is a fundamental property of personality. Some of us prefer chocolate to vanilla. Butter brickle gets others excited. If all of us thought alike we would forfeit our individuality.

Victims wait for the phone to ring to see who they are. The voice on the other end wants us to attend the Anti-lint League. Unable to turn it down, we show up to support another cause—that is not of our choosing.

I want to be me, and it's hard enough. Trying to be someone else is impossible.

Read the ministry of Jesus Christ. People tried to change Him. They hoped to get Jesus to switch causes or alter His plans. Choosing short pain, He told them no. He refused to be moved.

One example is when His brothers tried to get Him to go to Judea (John 7:1-9). They didn't care what happened to Him. If Jesus made a fool of Himself, they would have been all the happier.

Taking control of Himself, Jesus said no. The time wasn't right and He would be crazy to rush off into needless danger.

Jesus had to shape His personality by saying yes or no. We have to do the same.

3. *You gain reliability.*

People who can't say no often end up snowed. There are more good causes and great organizations than we have time or energy for. Our mail is filled with pleas and requests. We have school calendars, band calendars, church calendars, sports calendars, business calendars, social calendars. Someone should put all of them together into one guilt calendar!

By trying to keep up with everything, we're likely to disappoint everyone. The nice-guy image we were trying to project has turned into Mr. Dud. Mr. Unreliability. Soon people are carping behind our backs. Why did he take the job if he wasn't going to do it? All he had to say was that he didn't want it.

We break our backs and accomplish the exact opposite of what we hoped.

4. *You gain satisfaction.*

By picking which causes will demand our attention we greatly enhance our feelings of accomplishment. That's essential to feelings of self-esteem.

Select endeavors that you believe you can polish well, opportunities that will allow you to use your ample skills and talents. Why waste time as the servants of mediocrity? Others will try to tie us to the tasks they want done. As respectable as they might be, we would be far better off choosing the ones that seem to best fit our mix.

Those live best who live up to their own expectations. They are free to discover which exciting gifts God has given them (1 Corinthians 12).

Women in particular have special reason to evaluate their ability to say no. Some have fallen into ruts and can't see out.

Traditionally we have seen the female role as one of servitude. If someone asks women to serve they can hardly reject such a high calling. Can you bake cookies? Make new dresses for the band? How about centerpieces for the banquet tables?

The problem is that some women cannot turn down anything smacking of service. If it's service, they must take it.

Not true.

Women who refuse are not immoral.

Women who hate to bake are not scarlet.

Women who are not joiners are not brazen.

That's the point of the story of Mary and Martha. To have Jesus in their home was a big occasion. How do women react to big occasions? Martha was cooking, cleaning, tidying up, and hovering like a hummingbird.

Jesus called her up short. He wanted Martha to know there were other rich rewards in life. Drop the housekeeping and let's talk about God and the wonderful ways He works (Luke 10:38-42).

Women can bake cookies, but they don't have to. They can say no to service roles.

Many have lived in pain all their lives because they couldn't accept emancipation.

Of course there's an art to saying no. The blunt and the rude are seldom appreciated. In our chapter on Letting Others Down Easy we make suggestions on how to painlessly give them the axe.

If you're afraid of giving a no, you probably also

tremble at the thought of getting one. When we ask someone to help us, the same basic rules apply. We extend the identical privilege to say no that we treasure for ourselves.

A few quick guidelines if we're doing the asking.

Ask.

Don't say no for the person.

We want them to serve on the annual hunter's biscuit breakfast committee but we are afraid to ask. They seem terribly busy. Besides, they're rich and supposedly important.

It's too easy to argue with ourselves. Finally we conclude that they wouldn't want the job. But *they* should have the luxury of saying no. We should not say no for them. This task could be precisely what they've been dreaming of! Don't rob them of a thrill because you couldn't handle it.

Ask now.

Go for the short pain or quick lift.

By stewing over the thought of asking them, we usually make things worse. Grab the phone. Pick up the pen.

Why die daily? Procrastination is a slow torture. They can only say no once, but slowly wondering is a miserable death.

Ask clearly.

As a writer and speaker I get asked to do many things. That's part of the fun. Most of the things I turn down are because they were not presented clearly and directly.

Tell them what you want.

Tell them when you want it.

Tell them why you want them.

Tell them how long it will take.

If there is a fee included, tell them what you will pay or ask them what they charge. If you can't pay, tell them that.

Ask enthusiastically.

If it doesn't mean much to you, it won't mean much to them. Be spirited.

Recently I accepted the type of job I always turn down. Always. But this time I couldn't. The person who asked me was so wrapped up in what he wanted to do that I wanted to be part of it.

Ask humbly.

Humility and enthusiasm are not incompatible. If you feel the job is too important, it may frighten off the person you're asking. You really want the person, but the world will not end if he doesn't say yes. Get both messages across.

If your ego is on the line, you'll probably drop the ball. Be sincere and reasonable. His no is not an insult to your self-worth.

Ask others.

Is your project worthwhile or not? Does one rejection bring it to its knees? If so, something is wrong with the idea.

Victory often stands on a mound of rejections. With each rejection you could stand a little higher. When the right person is found you'll be happy you stuck it out.

When you're on the receiving end of a request, don't be afraid to think it over. Unless the answer is clear-cut, tell the person you'll get back to him. This gives you time to consult your calendar and your family, to pray, and to check other necessary areas. Maybe there's a birthday party that evening and you'll want to say no. Maybe there will be a piano recital that night and you will want to say yes!

Weigh the pluses and minuses. Get back to the person at the exact time you said you would. It's great to know you have been fair to everyone.

A friend called me from another state to ask me to speak. It didn't feel right, and yet he was a friend. Feeling uneasy, I asked him if I could call back.

I called when I said I would and explained my difficulty. I didn't feel right about speaking in that situation. But since he was my friend it was hard to say no. However, I needed to turn it down. If sometime he wanted to invite me down just to cook steaks, I'd love to come. Since he was my friend, I decided to use my best charm and to level with him.

It was hard, but I went for the short pain. I'm glad I did.

6

Deciding to Drop Out

Adios! Bon voyage! So long!

We feel that way sometimes, and we decide to take a hike. Under the right circumstances it's the perfect thing to do. We have to wonder why we didn't do it sooner.

Dropping out can be a sign of genuine maturity. But it can also indicate that we're afraid, uneasy, and retreating. How can we tell the difference? If we are withdrawing into a constricted, unhappy situation, we are heading in the wrong direction. But if bidding farewell is a step into optimism, we're probably on the right track.

Millions are so fearful of being rejected that they're bailing out of people encounters. Frequently what appears to be solitude is actually an attempt to avoid rejection.

Ann is the kind of girl who goes straight home after work and stays there. She reads during the evening, writes relatives, and goes to bed early. Nothing wrong with that. She is well-rested and ready for work in the morning.

That's fine if it's what one really wants. However, in Ann's case, she wishes she could be out. She wants to join a couple or group and laugh from the bottom of her feet. There is a wide gap between what Ann wants and what Ann does. The gap exists because she's afraid of being rejected.

To prevent being rejected, Ann does the rejecting for others. Afraid she'll be turned down by a group, she turns herself down. She feels that loneliness is less painful than moving about in society.

The number of Anns who are withdrawing is at a record high. According to some surveys the number has tripled over the past few decades. The reasons for this are worth noting.

1. When people are packed into close living and working conditions, they often reach for seclusion. The constant pressure of people makes many want to hide. Since they suffer through the risk of rejection during the day, they are relieved to escape that threat at night and over the weekends.

2. Mass communication tends to present other people as extremely good-looking, very prosperous, and highly mobile. If you feel you cannot fit into that picture, you are likely to retract yourself. Magazines and television sell the image of the nearly-perfect.

3. Breakdown of the family structure has led to much uncertainty and insecurity. It's bound to. Many of us move away from our extended families. These were the people who were supposed to accept us no matter what. We could have our car

repossessed or get fired at the plant, but we knew where we would be welcomed. Without an extended family, setbacks are as cold as concrete.

4. Divorce means that millions of people are drifting without a significant other person. They can't count on a hug when they get home.

Steve said, "I know I will get married again. I can't stand coming home to an empty house."

Since acceptance is not readily at hand, many people need to reach out to find it. But it's risky: Some will reach and others will withdraw. There is a chance of getting hurt.

With these social changes, more and more Anns are being created.

If a person wants to be alone, more power to him. Solitude is a healing, growing experience. It's a lost art for many of us who cannot stand silence.

The problem is that millions of people don't want to be alone. They're alone in agony. Their aloneness hurts.

Jesus understood the difference. Sometimes He wanted to be alone, but the pressing crowds made it nearly impossible. At times He had to get away with His disciples (Matthew 20:17-19). At other times He wanted to be by Himself (Luke 6:12). Yet Jesus also needed people and their support. When it wasn't available He felt greatly isolated (Matthew 26:40).

Everything in its time. If we're alone and we want to be with others, we're lonely. If we are lonely over a long period of time, we risk severe depression and other disorders.

A great deal of loneliness is created by *low*

self-esteem. We can't imagine why anyone would want to be with us. We're convinced we have little or nothing worth saying. We imagine our sense of humor to be inadequate. Before long we've persuaded ourselves that we're too ugly to tolerate.

That type of logic is like a gutter ball in bowling. Locked in, it can go but one place.

If rejection is the foregone conclusion, we work to make sure it comes true.

It's a form of self-defeat.

If the number of people who live alone and are lonely has tripled, what about the rest of the population? Even more people live with someone but feel generally rejected. At least 25 percent of those asked described themselves as withdrawn or lonely. That was their regular condition. Nearly half those surveyed reported frequently feeling lonely.

This seems verified by the huge number of gimmicks designed to bring people together. Not only are there singles' bars, dating clubs, and church groups, but there are also services to place born-again Christian men in contact with Philippine girls!

Magazines have mushroomed to cater to practically every taste, size, interest, and vocation of lonely people. Organizations exist to lower the risks and increase the probability of making friends in our society. In some cases this has worked wonderfully.

Those who use the resources available have decided to fight rejection. Cushioned in a more comfortable framework, they reach out to touch someone else.

Injured love is one of the major causes of loneliness. If you've been stung hard, you may not be eager to take more chances. Being rejected by someone you loved deeply is one of life's more severe emotional pains.

Having loved and lost, the wounded are likely to resort to unnatural behavior. They're likely to barricade themselves in their rooms or go dashing out to find another love. Either reaction is emotionally dangerous.

Those who search frantically for another person to love are trying desperately to fight rejection. Someone left them. Seldom are these departures executed with charm, poise, and wholesomeness. The people left behind usually feel dejected and worthless. They panic in their search for someone, almost anyone, to reaffirm their worth. Rushing into the arms of another person provides buoyancy to their ego: They are worthwhile again.

Normally this is a poor excuse for establishing a relationship. Often it turns out unhappy. That explains why the divorce rate among second marriages is so high. Many divorcees marry for reasons that can't hold them together over the long haul.

Those who marry to escape rejection frequently end up with double rejection.

The other extreme, determined to avoid this mistake, dive into bomb shelters. Seeking cover, they hope to escape the pain of another rejection.

The problem is that the fear of rejection leads to further rejection and multiplies the pain.

There are no bomb shelters safe enough to protect us from all emotional shock.

When a person withdraws because he thinks no one loves him, the fear soon becomes reality. His retreat causes others to reject him. Soon he gets stuck in a circle chasing his own tail.

He feels he is rejected, so he crawls into an emotional hole. Since he has crawled into a hole, no one can find him in order to love him. In his mind this proves the fact.

People who ask to be left alone normally are. A crisis arises because many people who ask for seclusion don't actually want it. They carry an aura of aloofness, but in their hearts they wish someone would swim the moat, scale the steep walls, and invade their life. They would like to lower the drawbridge and let you in, but they feel they can't. They seem to stand like steel, but inside they're cold and lonely.

Hardly anyone will climb a high, stiff wall.

If we shut others off, they assume we want to hold them out.

I see Zaccheus as a lonely, isolated person. His job, his money, and his reputation separated him from other people: Tax-collecting for an occupying government didn't draw affection from people!

Jesus had to scale the wall of this man's heart. He took the initiative and told Zaccheus that He was coming to have dinner at the publican's house (Luke 19:1-10).

The ministry of wall-scaling is a tough one, but its rewards are enormous. I have watched visitors attend church three or four times, sit in the back, and then never return. No one ever tried to scale their wall. There are others who tried to slip in and out on Sunday morning but someone headed them off at the pass. They were befriended warmly and pulled gently into the group.

Thank God for those who do not wait for the bridge to drop! They swim the moat and climb the wall.

Erv Nase did that for me. I used to attend a Christian youth group. Immediately after the meeting I would lunge for the door and escape into the night.

Erv decided to cut me off. He invited me to join the group for hamburgers and pop. The first couple of times I begged off and kept moving. Inside I wanted to go; I wanted to belong; I wanted to laugh with them. But I had to make sure I was wanted.

Finally I agreed to go, and I spent many years thoroughly enjoying that circle of friends. Thanks, Erv, for scaling my wall!

While this sometimes happens, it's unreasonable to expect it. If we go to the trouble of encasing ourselves in an ice palace, most people will assume we want to live there. Once they assume that, they will leave us alone.

The shame is that those who appear aloof often don't want separation. To protect themselves from pain, they've withdrawn. Few people are stuck-up. Very few consider themselves too good for others. Many more are afraid of getting hurt; that's why they keep their bridges closed.

Surprisingly, the age group suffering most from loneliness is the teenage-to-young-adult segment. They may appear to be having a great time, surrounded by caring friends, but surveys do not bear this out.

Part of the explanation may center on the changes going on in their lives. Their body is changing; their social status is in flux; their friends soon begin moving; they make decisions about love. Upheaval may best describe their turmoil.

With so many adjustments to make, there are many opportunities for rejection—new friends, new responsibilities, new schools, new jobs, new free-doms, new situations. That may sound exciting, but it could be *too* exciting. Trying to interpret each response as acceptance or rejection is a full-time job.

Lonely people have to make a decision: Will they live with loneliness or do they want to cure it? The cure takes one of two basic forms: We can hope someone will scale our wall or we can lower our bridge and let others in.

The first approach is risky. It's unreasonable to expect someone to burst through your fog and scale the wall. As nice as this sounds, it's terribly improbable.

Approach number two is where the odds are. If need be, painfully and slowly we have to lower the bridge and call others in. Complete with lights, warm fires, and open arms, we must encourage people to enter our space.

There are several suggestions to keep in mind for bridge-droppers.

1. *Expect some rejection.*

If you discourage easily you could be in big trouble. When you step out in trepidation the slightest movement might frighten you off. A frown, a hesitation, a quiver in someone's voice might be interpreted as rejection. We need to be constant in our openness to new friends. They might not accept an invitation at first, but they might the second or third time.

2. *You want people to like you, not love you.*

Some of us are asking for far too much. We fail to understand friendship. It doesn't mean someone becomes our twin. He or she isn't going to be around 24 hours a day. Thank heaven!

We are looking for someone to occasionally share with. We go to a ball game, play a little Trivial Pursuit, haul wood together. If it fits your mix you go shopping or take in a movie.

You get together once in a while because you enjoy each other's company. Many relationships fail because they are smothered to death. The Bible tells us that we can visit our neighbor too often and wear out our welcome (Proverbs 25:17). Great advice!

3. *Develop a circle of friends.*

It's possible to have a wide range of acquaintances but no friends. We don't need cliques aimed at excluding others. However, we could use a circle of dependable friends we can usually count on.

You may not all get together at once, but there are a handful of people you like to sit down with individually. When any of them walk into the room or you hear their voice on the phone, you brighten up.

There isn't enough time or energy to include whole armies in your portfolio of friends. You can't do that many friendships justice. Yet there is ample room for some special people.

Many of us become discouraged because we can't count our friends by the hundreds. Fortunate is the person who can count by five! Jesus collected

12 special people to surround Him. Of these, a mere three formed an intimate circle.

Zero in on a few friends. Keep those relationships fresh without smothering them. On a sad, rainy night they will be the ones that especially matter.

4. *Expect some bad times.*

Most friendships are like marriages: Some days you want to throw them out.

Everyone gets rude sometimes. Everyone is inconsiderate, boring, and demanding sometimes. Solid friendships hold on during the storms and come out stronger than before.

5. *Believe you can be a good friend.*

Relax. Give and take. Keep coming back. You can do it, and probably have done so many times.

As a human being created in the image of God, your potential for caring is enormous. A friend knows how to share and care. All of us can find other people who will respond to the way we share and care.

One of the most uncomfortable people is the one looking for an excuse to drop out of a group or a relationship. The feelings are dead. He now waits for a springboard to help him escape.

First we block off all avenues of possible healing. We stop talking to the person or cut conversation down to basics like "Do you have that report ready?" or "Pass the salt." If the relationship is less frequent, it soon becomes "Nice day."

We no longer make overtures that might accidentally open meaningful communication. Instead we are setting the person up. We are watching and listening for him to make a mistake. When he says something we can twist into an insult or an error, we will be ready to drop him.

At the point of bait-setting we become irrational. Our mate can make an otherwise-acceptable statement like, "We ought to buy new dining room furniture." Under less tension we would even agree with our spouse. However, under these circumstances we say, "She doesn't like the way we live."

In our minds we are looking for any hint of rejection—even an imagined hint. We will have little trouble finding it because we are predetermined to. In fact we *create* rejection!

We want to drop out of the relationship. Unable to take that assertive action, we make the person drop us. With that mental twist we force him between a rock and a hard place.

When a marriage partner decides he wants his wife to force him out, he may begin presenting impossible schemes. He may say he would like to see a marriage counselor. When she assures him that she is more than willing to seek help, he shrugs it off as insincere.

In his mind he has accepted her rejection. However, she actually did not reject him at all.

He might suggest that they take a trip to Europe to possibly revive their love in a vacation setting. When he presents the proposal he knows he isn't free to go. His job schedule won't allow the trip and his debts are entirely too tight.

Knowing that, why did he raise the possibility? He wanted her to verbalize why they couldn't go. Cunningly, he made her reject his totally unreasonable plan.

Normally this person would never act evilly. But in this situation he is dedicated to destruction. Unable to overtly reject her, he schemes to have her reject him.

It is possible for a person to wake up to what he is doing. If he does, he may choose to reopen the healing avenues. This begins by taking a careful survey of where his behavior is leading. Should he be unable to do that, he may need to ask a friend, counselor, or pastor for aid. Someone may be able to level with him and help stabilize his vessel.

Many of us have developed martyr complexes on similar reasoning: We have belonged to a group that has rejected our dreams; unwilling to separate ourselves from our suggestions, we begin to search for an exit.

We will not admit that we could not accept the rejection of our idea. Since all adults should be able to accept rejection, we change the issue to seem more mature. We attempt to build a case that proves they have rejected us personally.

The group or committee can't possibly win once we set them up. We rearrange practically all comments and actions into personal affronts. Most of us have done it.

We want to drop out but must create an excuse. The sly geniuses we are, this isn't even a major feat.

Solid friendship hangs close and doesn't look for schemes of rejection. It works at nurturing rather than slaying friendships.

The Bible tells us that a friend loves at all times (Proverbs 17:17). Friends don't play games which cause them to reject each other. Even during their low times they know that difficulties will pass and that their friendship will last.

Unfortunately, some people fail to recognize this principle and periodically purge their friends. They feel inadequate and unworthy. Afraid some friends have gotten to know them too well, they suddenly eliminate them.

This strange maneuver is based on our dislike for ourselves. Someone has seen our weaknesses and will not be able to cope with us. Therefore he must be removed. As painful as that is, we imagine it to be necessary.

Later we will haltingly enter another relationship which will eventually fall apart for the same causes. We will again decide to drop out.

This also explains why some of us drop friends as those friends expand their relationships. If our friend makes a new friend we may immediately drop out.

We may not want to compete with the new friends. Feeling inadequate, we are certain the new friends will reject us. Since we feel we aren't as good as others, we think our old friend will surely move away from us. We can't risk being rejected, so we beat them to the door. We drop our friend before he can drop us.

Trying to avoid pain, we frequently cause more.

Most of us—maybe all of us—are irrational at times.

The chilling reality is that most people who drop out do not want to. They found the relationship too painful to continue. However, what they wanted most was to feel accepted.

Afraid of being rejected, they looked for the exits. But their first choice would have been acceptance. They wanted to *feel* like they were appreciated.

While we struggle to acknowledge acceptance, we must begin with a sturdy foundation. We have been accepted by God through the Person of Jesus Christ.

Day in, day out.

Dirty, clean.

Stable, flighty.

Sane, crazy.

Calm, wild.

Calculating, irrational.

It's always the same with God. We are accepted. There is no need to drop out.

7

Accepting Yourself

Don was a superior salesman who traveled throughout the Midwest.

"It usually depends on me," he volunteered. "If I walk into an office dejected and feeling down on myself, it's almost always an unsuccessful call. I go a long way toward creating the atmosphere."

We can't totally control other people, nor should we be able to, but we are major contributors. If we smile at people, most of them will smile back. When we enter someone else's space and bring uncertainty with us, we have introduced tentativeness into his or her climate.

Transfer that scene to our families. If we come home grouchy or tense, this attitude spreads rapidly to other members of the tribe. Sometimes they clear out of our path. At other times their bad day openly clashes with ours.

Our inability to accept ourselves causes some people to reject our behavior. When we telegraph that we feel shaky about our ability, it causes others to feel shaky about us. This is especially true if they don't know us very well.

What does it mean to accept ourselves? Basically it is to like myself the way I am. That's the positive side. The negative side is refusing to believe I am superior or inferior. It includes admitting that I need improvement.

Acknowledging that you have a car is a statement of reality. You aren't bragging or making outrageous claims. You can then say that it needs new shocks and a battery. However, first you must acknowledge that you have a car.

Accepting ourselves is a simple declaration that we're legitimate people. We're good, bad, pudgy, thin, or bald. No matter what the qualifiers are, they do not alter the fact that we are complete. We are inferior to no one. We have no need to be superior to anyone. We are complete the way we are.

Once we have recognized the fundamental equipment, we can begin to admit our limitations and make adjustments. Accepting ourselves isn't false pride. It isn't denial of our need for improvement.

Accepting ourselves is making peace with ourselves. I'll never be quarterback for the Dallas Cowboys, but it's all right. I'll never speak eight languages, but it's all right. However, I will do things I like and I will stretch out to become better. And that's all right too.

Accepting ourselves is to make peace with God. We can't be angry with God about our size, hairline, I.Q., or ability to throw a Frisbee. We appreciate the way God has made us because we accept ourselves. We will work on the Frisbee toss later.

Accepting ourselves is to make peace with other people. We don't have to be jealous of what others do. She can sew better than you, but that's all right because you like what you do. You have come to terms with yourself.

This is precisely what Paul said about himself. He had learned that in whatever state he was, he could be content (Philippians 4:11-13). When he was in need, he didn't lash out at his own inadequacies. If goods were pouring in, the apostle wasn't crowing about his successes. Christ had helped him come to terms with himself. He had contentment.

Paul knew there was good and bad in his life. He knew that this was normal, and he had peace about it.

Not long ago we had a five-year-old black girl in our home. While she was playing with some black crepe paper she said matter-of-factly, "I hate black. I'm not black. I'm not a black person."

We don't pretend to fully understand everything she meant by that, but we do know that many preschool children hate the color of their skin. Some grow up to appreciate themselves. Others fight it all their lives. Accepting ourselves as ourselves is the beginning of a healthy relationship with the world around us.

If we refuse to accept ourselves, we will be at war with who we really are. By rejecting ourselves we leave a vacuum in our personality. If we refuse to declare ourselves adequate, we will launch a search for someone else to say we are acceptable.

That search will never end.

There is no person, there is no group, there is no regiment of people who will make us feel desirable until we accept ourselves. Nevertheless the chase goes on.

That search tends to distort life. If people do not make a sufficient fuss over us, we fear they've rejected us. Since they did not accept us—in the sense we wanted—we feel further diminished. This may not sound logical, but it works that way for many people.

Because a person did not enthusiastically accept us, our feelings are hurt. We will henceforth avoid such people.

Remember, this began because someone failed to enthusiastically accept us. That was his or her total crime.

This happens when the search for acceptance is the paramount drive in our lives. It becomes a distortion. Relationships become injured.

Our ability to accept ourselves takes the pressure off other people we meet. They can treat us with normal courtesy and not hurt our feelings. Relationships become more relaxed because we do not derive our sense of total worth from them.

No one can make up for our rejection of ourselves.

Self-acceptance is a vital key to preventing rejection by other people. It isn't a guarantee that we will avoid rejection (there are no such guarantees), but it is a clear deterrent.

Not only is the lack of acceptance a tragedy in relationships, but it leads to outrageous behavior. Much of our greed, adultery, pride, murder, and other vices are born in simple self-rejection. Because we are unhappy with what we are, we reach out to what others have.

The author of Proverbs (27:20) tells us that man's eye is never satisfied. We keep looking around at what others have and are seldom content with what we are.

Some people will protest that they have tried to accept themselves but have still suffered rejection.

Rejection is part of the human condition. As long as we are human, we will experience rejection. That doesn't make it a pleasant encounter, but it does prevent it from getting out of proportion.

The pouter simply believes the rejection should go away. It isn't fun or reasonable, so it shouldn't exist. Almost like a fairy tale, he chooses to believe in magic dust that removes unpleasantness.

Because we believe rejection can be avoided, many of us go to outlandish contortions to prevent it. Usually we make matters worse.

Those who are dedicated to eliminating rejection devise elaborate schemes. They do almost anything to appease almost everyone. In the process they compromise half of what they consider dear in life. They seldom disagree, hesitate to express their opinion, and generally deprive themselves. Mind you, it isn't being done out of some sense of Christian altruism: Their actions are dictated by fear; they can't risk being rejected in any sense of the word.

To dodge rejection, many people choose to tailor their activities. They guide their lives to sidestep any possibility of disapproval. Since this is impossible, their behavior is decidedly altered. Much of their energy is spent controlling their activities to prevent any risk of being turned down.

All of this is sad enough, but the final pain is yet to come: It can't be done. Human beings cannot escape rejection. Welcome to the human race!

By going to great gyrations to prevent rejection, in the final analysis we create more rejections. When we compromise all of our positions, when we abandon most human contacts, we generate perverted behavior. People with perverted behavior invite more rejection.

It's a little like running in order to stop sweating.

People are ingenious at developing schemes to escape rejection. Sometimes we dash to reject ourselves before anyone else has a chance to do it. It's a form of protective self-pity.

The "Don't call me dumb, I know I'm dumb" syndrome exists. If you say you can't bowl, it will save the embarrassment of having someone else say it. When you ask someone to play Ping-Pong you frequently hear a self-rejecting litany: "Oh, I haven't played it in a couple of years," or "I don't know if I can play with these shoes," or "Boy, my back is acting up but I'll give it a try."

It's a ritual as old as table tennis. We are setting ourselves in position to soften the rejection in case we play poorly. Defeat doesn't hurt as much if we admit it before we start. Should we win, it will double the victory. After all, we predicted humiliation!

We could call this "the race to rejection." If we confess to being inferior, we will stop others from enunciating the thought.

This practice might seem harmless in table tennis, but what of those who spread it across their lives? "The dinner isn't much," or "I'm not a very good friend," or "I don't read very well." The list of self-defacing recitations is endless.

What we want is for the person to contradict us. Hopefully he or she will beg to differ and insist that this is the greatest dinner since the invention of chicken. Afraid the compliments might not come, we cover ourselves with derogatory remarks.

Either goal is demeaning: Begging for accolades lacks dignity, but so does the need to deface ourselves.

Many people who have rejected themselves have diverted their energies into helping other people. What could be wrong with that? If you are having some personal problems, it frequently helps to get lost in alleviating the needs of others.

Sound good? *Forget it!*

Didn't Jesus tell us to deny ourselves and take up our cross and follow Him (Matthew 16:24)?

To deny yourself of things, time, and pleasures in order to help others is commendable. To deny your worth, your dignity, is a drastically different concept.

The only happiness some people will accept is vicarious: They work to make others happy but do not consider themselves worthy of the same pleasure. It can be seen readily in many parents. They give the young people the car, fill it with gas, buy them clothing, and sacrifice greatly to guarantee a good time. That appears sane unless the parents could not do the same for themselves. Some people can find happiness only in making others happy.

This type of self-rejection can be an express ticket to a divorce court. The parents didn't do things together—not for each other and certainly not for themselves. Everything was done to make others happy.

Accepting ourselves recognizes that we have legitimate needs that must be met. Happiness is one of those basic needs. If our needs are met, we are better able to reach out and lend a hand to others in need.

Contrary to total-denial philosophies, there are many good things in life to which we are entitled. We deserve them on the basis that we are human beings. There are some things we have earned and deserve to keep. There are other things, like air and water, which have been given to us by God and are rightfully ours.

We are not nothing!

Resist any dogma or doctrine which teaches we are nothing.

We can think!

Denounce any school of thought that teaches we cannot trust ourselves to think. We certainly cannot trust anyone else to think for us!

When you read the Bible, take note of how much individuality God allows. He lets people succeed and He permits failure. When men wrote the books of the Bible through God's inspiration, God nevertheless let them express their own styles and personalities. God did not reject individualism, and neither must we.

Many people are afraid that if they begin accepting themselves it will go too far. Before long they might even enjoy themselves, and soon they will become proud, even arrogant.

On the contrary, genuine self-acceptance will defeat pride and not promote it.

Recently I have been noticing the ages of some young executives. Several 30-year-olds are presidents of companies. I'm in my middle forties and haven't even become president of a Sunday school class! As if that isn't depressing enough, I heard about a 24-year-old self-made millionaire. I own an 11-year-old Dodge!

How do we survive with that kind of news being pumped across our television sets? Many people don't. They're out trying to match every success story they have ever heard. The sad thing is that there's no end to it: We will always find someone who has done better in one way or another.

Self-acceptance is our deliverance. When we become happy with who we are, we are more likely to be happy with what we have. Working to accomplish, we are not driven to conquer.

We are then able to discover the lost harbor of humility. Humility offers us shelter when the storms of competitive greed roar against us. Humility keeps us secure when others are running in all directions after another 24-hour fad.

In the parable of the workers in the vineyard (Matthew 20:1-16) Jesus seems to be addressing the problems of envy and humility. Some workers complained that they had not been paid as much as others. However, insisted the employer, they were paid what they had agreed to, and it was a fair wage. Why then do we drool over what others receive?

It's endless!

Comparing ourselves to others is death to our own fulfillment. Contentment is impossible.

The problem of self-esteem is not that we are missing basic equipment or gifts: We have what we need; the fear is that we don't have what others have.

A great stumbling block is carrying too much luggage from the past. We have real and imagined regrets. The ghosts of yesteryear shackle us. We rattle through life dragging the chains of mistakes. These manacles hold us down and create pain for decades. But if we refuse to forget the past we sacrifice the present and the future.

Cut yourself free. Pat yourself on the back. Buy a new shirt. Get tickets to a concert.

Many people feel shadowed by an accuser. Whenever we try to accept ourselves, that mystical character points its crooked finger and calls out, "But don't forget you are this and you did that." His charges hold us in prison.

We must challenge the accuser. Whatever yesterday was like, it will not rob our tomorrows. We will seize liberty.

I wish I knew more about Satan and his role in human dilemmas. For some of us he could be the accuser (Revelation 12:10). If so, he obeys a sharp rebuke and a brisk dismissal. Tell him to take a hike and the charlatan will run away (James 4:7).

However you explain the accuser, the effect is

real: Thousands of people wilt under its effect. It must be resisted chin-to-chin, nose-to-nose. The accuser will depress you if it can. The only way it can is if you accept the attacks without resistance.

We will listen to no more charges. There will be no more lists of past mistakes, no more pain from blunders we have made.

Christ invites us into the bright sunshine of today.

I have met people who are still bitter because they weren't selected cheerleader in high school. Twenty years later they are either pouting about it or else pushing their daughter to succeed. Unable to accept the fact that today they're 40, they are still trying to justify what happened.

Men watch football wondering why they were never good enough to be the local hero. Instead of letting go and following adult pursuits, they still agonize over adolescent failures—at least they're perceived as failures.

We must stop rearranging yesterday. First, because it can't be done. Second, because we don't remember it as accurately as we might imagine. Third, because it prevents us from grabbing the important things of today.

8

Reducing
Your Frustration

If frustration is great and lasts for a considerable time, you can expect an outburst. It has to blow up internally or externally. Keep that in mind as you inventory your frustration.

A prime example is Jesus Christ. His outburst over the moneychangers in the temple demonstrates how wide the gap was. Their ability to degenerate the house of God into a money-making circus rested light-years away from what God intended. When Jesus was unable to shorten the gap between what should have been and what was, His frustration erupted in anger (John 2:12-22).

This story tells us several things about frustration:

1. It happens to the best of us.
2. It isn't necessarily wrong.
3. Great frustration can result in outbursts.

There are times when all of us should become angry—angry at starvation, at war, at injustice, at prejudice. But anger out of control soon becomes destructive.

By controlling our frustrations we help control our anger. It's not that we have swallowed our anger. Rather, by reducing our frustration, we shrink our need for anger.

Frustration is the gap between what you want to happen and what actually goes on. If a wide gap exists over a long period of time, anger and all its trappings are bound to result.

Most mothers would like their babies to behave in an orderly way. Since babies often refuse to cooperate, the mother is predestined for frustration. She expects the baby to cry, but after it's changed and fed she expects it to simmer down.

If the baby persists in crying, the mother's frustration gap widens. She tries all she knows but the crying refuses to abate. The wide gap between her wishes and reality remains, possibly for hours.

Frustration turns to anger. Anger may then collapse into spanking, beating, and abuse. An otherwise-loving mother couldn't reduce the frustration gap.

Repeated rejection is bound to give birth to frustration.

Sustained frustration is bound to give birth to anger.

Sustained anger is bound to give birth to destruction—either internal or external.

If that anger remains, it turns to bitterness.

Should bitterness remain, it turns to depression.

Depression gives birth to a full litter of problems.

All of this being the case, we must reduce the frustration which rejection brings.

Our major goal will be to narrow the frustration gap by cutting down on our rejection.

To do this we set up targets that we will hit with a reasonable amount of accuracy.

How many people have read a "You can do anything you want" book only to set themselves up for failure? By taking three or four chances at once, they multiplied the possibility that they would fall. Fortifying themselves with pep talks but little preparation or substance, they rose on a pedestal guaranteed to tumble.

By continuously aiming at unreachable goals and by facing rejection from clients and employers, their frustrations only mount. Eventually anger also accumulates as they search for people to blame their disasters on.

If we find ourselves in a situation that produces more frustration than it does satisfaction, we must reevaluate our circumstances. What changes can be made that will increase our ratio of accomplishments? Should we fail to make those adjustments we could be heading for irrational or destructive behavior.

Many divorces can be explained by a series of frustrations. The number of favorable strokes did not compensate for the large amount of agony. When the emotional ledger continuously failed to balance, the person decided to bail out.

A marriage might be rescued if the couple could help narrow the frustration gap. They can't eliminate all differences, but they can make the gap smaller.

Human beings don't handle frustration well.

Because of this fact, families, organizations, businesses, churches, and other relationships are ruined. We must temper frustration by bringing hopes closer to actuality.

This explains why many people in inner-city slums have chosen to burn buildings, rob homes, and strip cars. They cannot turn even modest dreams into reality. Denied common hopes, their frustration turns to anger and anger to outburst.

Frequently the official reaction is to prevent outbursts by stricter law enforcement. But to a few people the true solution is evident: We must narrow the frustration gap.

In similar fashion we insist that the church become more outspoken against the growing problem of divorce. But other people aim at reducing the pressures that create marital friction.

Our personal lives will become less hostile if we increase the amount of our satisfaction and fulfillment. How can we decrease the frequency of rejection?

Let's weigh a few suggestions.

Surround yourself with a large number of satisfying experiences.

It may be true that we grow through adversity, but we also grow through success. If we are overwhelmed by rejections, our personalities can soon become badly bruised.

Put yourself into low-risk situations. If you bowl well, do it. If you like to water ski, buy equipment. It's too easy to move toward hostile environments. Reinforce your self-esteem with rewarding practices.

We each have things we love to do. Maybe we've

drifted from the things that were genuinely satisfying. All of us need to increase that ratio of satisfaction.

Take calculated risks.

For me to agree to sing would demonstrate brain rot. Why would I ask for pain? Why would I invite rejection? Yet in a self-destructive way, many of us do this very thing.

We need to try enough new things to cause our lives to stretch. But to make it all a risky business could hurt our feelings of security. Pick out three or four chancy but hopeful ways to grow. To jump into too many ways at once is asking the building to fall in on you.

Evaluate your present situation.

Can you win where you are? If not, why don't you go where you can? Many people know they're in over their heads. They're undertrained, underpaid, undermotivated, underequipped, and underappreciated. They're just under.

Are you sure you want to spend the next decade frustrated?

Subtract and add.

Don't leave life's improvements to chance. Keep adjusting your experiences. Throw a frustration out today. Pick up a satisfaction. If the number of miserable situations gets out of hand, you could find yourself putting a fist through a lemon meringue pie—or worse.

Take note of your trends.

If your attitudes are changing, which way are they going? Are you more hostile this month or less? Have you noticed growing bitterness?

Are you sinking into a distaste for life?

Have you noticed an upswing in your disposition? Are you laughing a bit more? Can you see the humor in muddy shoes or a flat tire?

All of us have bad incidents. It's the bending of the twig that needs to be watched.

Frustration doesn't have to do us in. Sometimes it becomes the cannon shot to greater things. Richard Kopelman studied baseball players who had been traded. In their first year after the trade they batted well against the club that had let them go—almost 20 points higher.

Their reaction against rejection was funneled into productivity. At first their self-esteem was injured, but they reacted in a positive, socially accepted manner.

Not all of us use such laudable methods.

Trapped by frustration, most of us try to lunge out at its cause. That's why a fired worker might go back and shoot up the factory. He feels a need to hurt whatever he thinks caused his misery. Not only is it destructive, but often it's vented against the wrong people.

If we aren't invited to a party, we may hate the person who left us off the list. He rejected us. We were pronounced as unworthy for his social gathering.

Instead of saying "Who cares?". . . instead of admitting that we can't be invited everywhere. . . instead of accepting this as a natural part of life. . . we become frustrated. We then might hate the person who rejected us. Possibly we will choose to no longer speak to him.

Trying to get even, we strike out because we've been rejected. To do it we may try to hurt someone.

When we start down this path, we flirt with great danger. Not only are we threats to other people, but we are prone to do ourselves tremendous harm.

In the study of Type A and Type B behavior related to heart disease, researchers found that one emotion was more damaging than all others *combined*: hostile feelings. In the study hostilities were free-floating and covered a wide category of people. Hostility puts a lot of pressure on the human heart.

Maybe Jesus was aware of this when He told us to love our enemies (Matthew 5:43-48). If we go through life half-ticked, we put great pressure on ourselves. By loving those we thought may have wronged us, we relax our physical system as well as temper interpersonal relationships.

Jesus became frustrated (Matthew 23:37-39) much like the rest of us. He also knew some basic ingredients to help Him go with the punches.

In order to combat frustration, some authorities on human behavior have gone to dangerous extremes. They have concluded that since frustration is our problem, we need to get rid of it. If the need for a new car frustrates us, we should get a new car. If we are irritated by our lack of new clothing or feel deprived because we can't vacation in France, we must be gratified. To deny ourselves is to tempt discomfort and anger.

Nonsense! Frustration is a normal part of life. The fact that we live with other people guarantees frustration. Solutions are found in controlling frustration to a manageable level.

This form of anxiety is found in any perfectionist or would-be perfectionist. A great distance must exist between his dreams of grandeur and stark reality. To maintain the myth he must keep jockeying for position. How can he avoid situations which will prove he isn't perfect? How can he continuously seek the light that will show his best side?

Aiming for a fantasy existence drains our resources. Drained resources end in anger.

This is a persistent problem for young adults (and older) who are still trying to please elderly parents. Their parents have made it plain that they expect perfection from their child.

No matter what the child has done, his parents have pointed out whatever is not perfect. "But what about this spot?" or "It could be a little neater." It's a no-win situation.

When the child became an adult, the nit-picking correcting continued. As principals, lawyers, bank presidents, professors, or Marine sergeants, they still get rejection from their parents.

They cannot please their parents. Frustration turns to anger.

Many cannot verbalize their feelings, but they run deeply: They are angry. Yet they feel they aren't supposed to be angry at their parents. They have become doubly frustrated. Forced to become angry, they are at the same time denied the right to be angry.

This explains why we express displaced anger. Unable to be angry at the real target, we find other victims to dump our anger on them. Children are frequently the victims of misplaced anger. They place a toy in the wrong part of the room and suddenly suffer a terrible chewing-out. Little can they know that the parent is actually angry at someone else!

Confused and bewildered, the child becomes frustrated. How do you please a parent who has lost all rationality? The child in turn becomes angry and must find a place to vent that feeling. Some learn to throw their anger back at the parent. Others turn it loose on siblings, friends, or pets. Too many feel forced to swallow it and direct their hostility inward.

Human beings create problems for other people because of their failure to handle their own difficulties. Wives, husbands, and children are torn apart by someone else's frustration.

The people we love deserve better treatment.

As loving individuals we can help by a few positive steps. One of the best is to simply tell our family what is bothering us. When we come into the house barking, snapping, and impatient, we create chaos. Usually the family will give us a wide path as soon as they detect our mood. However, they frequently get mowed over by our miserable disposition.

To be fair, we need to be up front about our problems. Announce immediately that you're mad at the grocer. Tell them the boss is a muttering idiot. Each of us deserves an explanation when someone we care for is treating us like dirt.

We also make life easier for others if we discuss

our frustration with the person who is causing it. It's our obligation to protect our family by confronting the real problem. Otherwise those close to us suffer from the fallout.

We're prone to hurt our family before we risk confronting someone else. It's no wonder some families are run like asylums!

We can furnish stability by pulling our dreams within the realm of possibility. If we live on the edge of perpetual frustration, other people get knots on their heads because of our troubles.

Since frustration is man's lot, we need to find constructive ways to release our tension. Imperfect people living among an assortment of neighbors, working for illogical organizations, filling out unintelligible tax forms, watching indefensible television shows, hearing incomprehensible sermons, reading inconceivable plots, and paying inexhaustible bills will leave the best of us somewhat nutty.

Those who cannot find socially acceptable outlets for their frustrations are likely to cause trouble. They seek prostitutes, gamble, or possibly drive themselves into unmanageable debt. Their goal may be to get control over their lives and their situation. Often the result is further calamity.

Frustrated individuals often tend to overdo things in order to compensate. They tend to overeat, overdrink, overreach, overreact, overtalk, or overexercise. Fleeing, they're trying to forget whatever prevents them from fulfilling their dreams.

Happy are those who discover volleyball, swimming, walks in the park, and skating. They too seek outlets.

Unchecked and undiverted frustration will lead some of us to retaliate against those whom we feel caused our problem. In many cases that person is innocent, but we perceive him as rejecting us and our ambitions.

If we want to join a yacht club but can't afford the membership, we might become angry at the members. When we stay angry, we might want to get even by refusing to buy at their stores or attend their churches. In our limited way we are trying to retaliate for something which may not be their fault at all.

This is another place where the gospel moves in to help calm us down. It will not allow us to get into the business of getting even. We are preserved by the steady love that tells us not to hate others. The love of God holds us in check from leaning toward irrational hate (1 John 4:20).

Envy creates enormous grief. Keeping our frustrations to a manageable level produces overall peace.

9

Did Your Parents Reject You?

A significant percentage of the population has trouble handling any form of rejection because they were rejected as children by their parents. They still feel the insecurity created by that experience. For them it is the dominant theme in life. They fail to get a grip on today because they are unable to understand yesterday.

If you don't suffer from this, you probably know someone who does.

Before we discuss how that happens, we must dispel a myth. It's easy to find a scapegoat and blame everything on our parents. This approach has been overdone.

Some of us want to believe our parents rejected us. By believing that we can sweep all our idiosyncrasies into one pile. We imagine we are poor, fat, impatient, in debt, bearded, and delinquent in our taxes because of our parents. In most cases that bird won't fly.

Even with the best of parents we generally adopt

our own peculiar foibles. We select our own defense mechanisms, create our own brand of heroes, set our own goals, and drive to fulfill our own particular image.

Parents can't become crutches to carry all our weaknesses.

Having said this, the fact remains that some adults are in terrible shape, and it began with rejection from their parents.

To simplify the matter we need to divide parental rejection into two basic forms: overt rejection and covert rejection.

Overt rejection is severe, but it's not always the worst. This means a parent said he didn't like the child and supported that statement with actions. This parent didn't leave much to guess about.

Nine-year-old children have been driven to hospital waiting rooms and left. The parents drove off for another state and were never heard from again.

Thirteen-year-old girls have been told to gather up their clothing and leave. They were told to never return. Their physical parents were finished with them.

Actions like this don't leave much room for discussion. The child isn't trying to figure out what the parent meant: It's final. He or she may be bewildered over why it happened, but he knows what happened.

A second category of overt rejection is the live-in variety. A parent says, "I wish you had never been born," or "You've never brought me anything but grief." That's rejection when it is backed up by rejecting behavior. The parent doesn't talk to the child, except gruffly; he doesn't meet his physical needs, except briskly. A relationship doesn't exist.

Those who are *covertly* rejected, on the other hand, have never been told so in precise words; they've been left to draw their own conclusions.

Covert rejection can be more painful than overt. The child is left hanging, with nothing to grab onto. His parents never say they don't love him, but their actions say exactly that.

He is getting a message, but he doesn't know how to interpret it.

Children can hardly comprehend a parent rejecting them. They see the parent image as knowing, wise, capable, and generally correct. Most children who believe in Santa Claus do so because an adult told them it was true.

A child wants to feel secure, loved, and wanted by his parent. It's a natural need. When the child begins to sense rejection, he will resist those feelings. He wants to believe the best; he *needs* to believe the best.

That's part of what makes sexual abuse so horrendous: The child wants to believe the best about adults, and particularly about his parents.

Into the accepting mind of a child come messages of rejection. He is confused, even shocked. He senses a lack of love in the form of caring. Parents don't act like they love him.

His basic emotional needs are not met because his parents have pushed them aside. He has no one to talk to about the big dog down the street. The school music teacher has asked him to wear white shirts on Thursday. The child doesn't know if his parents will take care of that. There's a general sense of not caring which permeates the child's life. He may not be able to identify the feelings as rejection, but he detects a lack of caring. When he continuously believes that no one cares, the child begins to develop an aura of hopelessness.

This may explain why some children survive poverty better than others. Those with little money but caring parents often learn to cope. But no money and no care is a combination which leaves scars.

We should not confuse this with normal complaints. Practically every child says that no one cares what happens to him. That's just self-pity. All of us suffer from it. It comes and goes in spurts.

The serious problems are among those who have a deep-seated conviction of rejection. It doesn't ebb and flow. Such children are constantly convinced that no one cares, and yet they remain in residence with their parents.

These relationships maintain a destructive ambivalence. A child knows he should love his mother, and yet there is little reciprocation. What's a child to do? He can't totally write off his parents, but neither can he draw close to their acceptance.

Frequently this results in torturous self-rejection by the child. Why don't his parents like him? He soon becomes persuaded that there must be something wrong with him.

For years, even decades, he may go through the rejection swing. One day he blames his parents for rejecting him. The next day he turns it on himself and calls himself simply unlovable. He believes that if he were the least bit lovable his parents would surely have loved him.

Rejected children are often in for a lifetime of conflict.

The children of divorce frequently find themselves in a similar dilemma. A supposedly caring parent moves out. Before he leaves he reassures the child that their relationship will be special. They love each other. He will soon have her over to his new place. They will have great times together. There's nothing to worry about.

During the first month her father pops in a couple of times for trips to the zoo, maybe to an amusement park. The next month he returns once. There is no visit the third month. He's gone, possibly never to return.

Why did he do that? Does he really love her? Is there something wrong with her? Why has she been rejected?

When these girls and boys become adults they are often still asking the same questions. Why did the parent who moved out reject them?

This isn't merely an interesting childhood problem. Many rejected children grow up to become rejecting parents. They get into a cycle that they don't know how to break. The only parenting model they have seen up close has been one in which the parents rejected the child. They are therefore prone to repeat part of that style.

The good news is that not everyone gets caught in that trap. Identifying what has happened to them, they are determined to rescue their own children from rejection. Carefully they keep correcting themselves when they see the temptation to reject their own children. Sometimes the children of rejection become among the best parents. However, this is not accomplished easily.

Education, counseling, self-help, and a loving spouse contribute greatly to breaking the generational cycle. Few remedies are as effective as creating a happy atmosphere at home. Laughter, games, and sharing go a long way to erasing temporary feelings of rejection. Consciously cutting back on poor attitudes will help make our children know they are welcome with enthusiasm.

There are certain key emotional factors that show themselves in some adults who felt rejected as children. By understanding them we will be better able to combat their effect.

Do you expect rejection?

If we have experienced rejection from childhood we also expect it now. We consider ourselves highly rejectable. When we meet someone, we believe he is almost predestined to reject us. We look for any frown or halting tone. If the person gives any clue, we imagine it as confirmation that he has rejected us.

What a relief! We knew he would reject us, and we're right.

We are more comfortable at reading rejection because we have more practice at it. In most cases we reject acceptance. We are adroit at turning compliments into insults.

Before we meet a person we tell ourselves he will reject us. And why not? We have seen most encounters as rejection.

Do you feel like an "other"?

"Other" means that we believe we are basically different. By repeated and early rejection we have grown to believe that other people are not like us. The setbacks that we face would not happen to someone else. But for some strange reason they do fall on us.

Mark explained his feelings this way: "I can't stand to meet new people. The minute I walk into a room I know everyone will dislike me. They can see an ugly side of me that I can't see. It's hard to describe, but you know it's going on."

Repeated rejection turns into imagined rejection. Now we have trouble telling the difference.

Do you feel touchy?

Since we expect to be rejected and since we are continuously trying to interpret what other people say, we soon find ourselves extremely touchy. There is no end to examining what others say. If she says she likes our tie we interpret that to mean she doesn't like our coat. If we are invited to play tennis on Tuesday, we wonder why he left us out when he plays golf on Saturday.

Touchiness doesn't necessarily come from vanity or conceit. It could be caused by our search for ourself. Acceptance is a foreign concept that leaves us ill-at-ease. Rejection is an old friend, an old shoe. We feel more comfortable with its discomfort.

It's hard to maintain a friendship with someone who is touchy. Given anything but a crystal-clean, positive statement, the person rejected from his childhood will turn it into a rejection.

These are difficult feelings, and many people

need in-depth counseling to begin overcoming it. Others have been able to gain a form of self-respect by going gently to their adult parents and establishing an equal, one-on-one relationship. Not recommended for everyone, some differences have been conquered in this way.

No longer parent-child, they now talk on an even plane. Some have found a peace with each other that they never had at home.

This may explain why some adopted children later want to go back and find their physical mother. They would like to know why they were let go. Hopefully they will hear a noble explanation. They want to hear why their mother couldn't keep them and that she gave them up with great love. Hearing this, they expect to feel free. They will know they were not rejected because of who they are.

All of us want to know this regardless of our circumstances.

We then dedicate ourselves to breaking the cycle. Our children will not know the rejection that was ours. Deliberately we coat our children with love and acceptance. Like rust protection, we hope to save them from the terrible agony that rejection by parents can bring. Fortunately, the cycle of rejection can be broken. We *can* have secure, confident children who feel loved and wanted.

10

Preparing Children for Acceptance

When you make a child feel he's special to you, you've given one of the greatest gifts in life—no doubt about it. Children who feel they're special to no one have problems accepting themselves.

But first let's explain "special."

Special means you like them tremendously and would deeply miss them if they were gone. There's a spot in your life that they fill, and you like the way they fill it.

It doesn't mean they're going to be a great athlete, President of the United States, a movie star, or an astronaut. Special doesn't refer to performance or talent.

Special doesn't refer to good and bad behavior. We like them when they fail, when they forget, and even when they lie. They don't have to live in constant fear that they will lose favor with us.

Nor does it have anything to do with comparisons. We don't think they're special because they are cuter, politer, faster, quieter, or more helpful than someone else. They don't have to fear that someone even cuter will come along and displace them. To make them feel they're better than others is a disservice which will catch up with them.

We don't mean that special is different, either. They aren't special because they sit in a wheelchair or are missing a hand. The fact that they have trouble with numbers or can't pronounce Massachusetts isn't what makes them special.

The word "special" is misused and frequently becomes an ugly adjective. In its best context the word has an unmatched strength.

Special means you like them tremendously and would miss them if they were gone. If a person not only hears this but feels it, he is halfway home to accepting himself. Those who never feel it are in for a hard struggle.

The great part about making someone feel special is that practically anyone can bestow it. Parents may convey it best, but they aren't the only ones who carry this magic.

Grandparents have a way of making a young person feel like the National Anthem. They all but stand up and salute him when a child comes in the room. Uncles and aunts also carry this magic.

Many of us were made to feel accepted by school teachers who communicated genuine interest in us. Neighbors, playground directors, Sunday school teachers, coaches, Scout leaders, and ministers can have a peculiar talent for making other people feel like a million dollars.

Each of us needs someone who loves having us around. We find it easier to accept ourselves because we know someone else accepts us.

The University of Nebraska came up with six factors which make a strong family. One of those elements was that each member of the family knew that if he were gone, he would be missed. He filled a gap where no one else could completely fit.

If we want to prepare children for balanced lives we need to supply them with that special feeling of acceptance. As we reinforce that feeling, we give them the strength to handle rejection.

How do we enable a person to stand up under rejection? Some people believe you give him rejection and make him tough. When the wind blows he will be strong enough to hold on.

That analogy falls apart. We don't strengthen buildings by exposing them to as much wind as possible; rather, we build them strong enough before we let the wind run wild.

To stand against rejection a child needs solid reinforcement by acceptance. Ten good experiences will make him secure enough to resist one bad one. Ten bad experiences do not necessarily make him strong enough to hold under number eleven.

By letting a child know he's special and giving him good, reassuring experiences, we prepare him to face rejection. It's a noble service worthy of the angels.

When asked what accounted for her stability, a lady replied, "My mother considered me a gift from God. All of us felt her love and faith in us. I always thought I could do anything I set out to do because my mother thought I could."

There's no way to guarantee the behavior of a

child. However, the prophet Samuel had a mother who dedicated her child to God. She said, "I prayed for this child, and the Lord has granted me what I asked of him" (1 Samuel 1:27 NIV).

Heavy gratitude!

Compare these scenes to the large number of women who are sorry they are mothers. In surveys the percentage of mothers who regret the experience is staggering. Not only is the mother unhappy, but she is bound to pass that misery on to her child. The child will in turn find life extra difficult.

Many mothers are aware of the potential problem and to their credit have changed their attitudes. This is no small accomplishment, but women are doing it, much like catching themselves in midair.

They realize that they did not want the child. They admit that the child creates a financial and emotional hardship. Yet thousands of mothers have decided to abandon their self-pity and concentrate their love on their child. Some are heroic efforts.

Consequently, the fact that a child was not "planned" doesn't mean he's rejected. From that initial regret often arises a total encompassing love for the child. Some "late" children, some "early" children, some "inopportune" children, some children of a single parent are among the most appreciated.

Not that the crux of this matter rests only on mothers. Fathers supply equal negative and positive reinforcement. When a father cannot grapple with being a father he leaves profound negative feelings with his children.

A father who shows patient interest in his child

adds enormously to the attitude of worthiness and acceptance. Attending plays in the garage, listening to original stories, and swinging on a rope in the backyard are part of fortifying that child.

In our mad rush to purchase educational toys we may be reaching for the wrong goals and accidentally hitting the correct ones. The most important reason why we play Scrabble is *not* to help them with their spelling. By playing games we tell the child we like him. He is worth spending time with. We enjoy being close. Spelling may come easier because the child feels important, but the feeling of significance is far and away the more vital of the two.

Fathers who are too busy for their children indicate their priorities (as do busy mothers). Hunting, clubs, jobs, trips, and committees are more important than the child if they prevent that father from furnishing adequate time with the child.

The conclusion is inevitable, and children catch on quickly. They learn where they fit on the list of activities. That's a value judgment, and they learn to evaluate it.

Many children grow up to be emotionally handicapped because they were emotionally abandoned by their fathers (or mothers). When a child colors a picture and feels good about his work, he wants to share that joy with someone else. If he is continuously prevented from sharing that happiness, he is forced to retract that joy.

No big deal—all of us have to do that occasionally. The real rub comes when the child is repeatedly denied that pleasure. He is robbed of an emotional outlet.

This frustration is far worse if the child knows that his father is well, available, and near but chooses to do other things. He doesn't have time for his child's emotional releases.

A child needs the outlet for both positive and negative emotions. Who does he talk to about the big dog down the street? Who will listen to the nightmare that bothers him?

Children feel deeply. If they cannot find acceptable ways to express those feelings, they may stop expressing them. Other children will finally burst and display emotions which indicate their severe pain.

Birthdays, promotions, recitals, plays, games, science shows, and craft displays cannot be totally ignored by a parent who could be there. A child begins to add up his value under that system. If it tallies against him, it can result in emotional handicaps.

Naturally someone raises the objection that a child could be smothered by too much attention. It's a valid point.

Those who hover over their children, tending to each tear and turning every mud pie into a national celebration, need to air out a little. Children learn little emotional freedom attached to an umbilical cord.

Too much freedom, as too much closeness, can result in a child who has trouble sharing his emotions. Emotions need to be vented in safe, secure surroundings.

Let's remind ourselves again: There is no way to guarantee the behavior or personality of a child. It's not a mathematical formula. Don't assume that adults who have troubles were mistreated or neglected as children. Each of us experiences a multitude of variables.

Our job is to give it our best shot, to give a child all the emotional advantages we can supply. Don't throw boulders in his way. There are enough nuts, psychotics, pimps, pornographers, racists, tyrants, and screwballs on the loose to provide plenty of heartaches for everyone. We owe it to our children to create as much emotional stability as possible.

In many of the situations we have been discussing, children have suffered rejection on general principles. A parent may not dislike that particular child, but simply have no room for children in general. He would treat another child just as indifferently. It's child neglect of an impersonal nature.

Horrendous at best, it is a separate category from specific rejection. Specific rejection says, "I don't like this child. If it were another child, I might enjoy him."

Specific rejection comes in different degrees, ranging from total disassociation to general dislike. There are many reasons why a parent might not be fond of his child. In some cases the parent recognizes the feeling but has not yet identified its cause. By raising a few possibilities we might jar loose some hidden feelings.

There are parents who have not accepted their child because she is a girl. This feeling is not as uncommon as we might like it to be.

A father related that when the nurse walked into the waiting room she said, "Congratulations! Would you like to see your daughter?" He remembers his reaction as, "Well, I guess." He hadn't thought about having a girl.

The feeling of being tolerated is easily transmitted, especially after the boy is born and the girl is virtually ignored. There are miles between being accepted and being tolerated.

This feeling is intensified when the parents attempt to make her into a boy. Clearly disappointed, they dress her, name her, involve her, and treat her in a way that lets her know she is being programmed to supplement for a missing male. She lives with rejection.

Disappointment with a daughter only begins the list. How many parents wish their boy had been a girl? How many wish their intellectual had been an athlete? They wish their child could shine on the playing field as a reflection of his talented parents.

How many parents wish their child could get a Ph.D. as evidence of the parents' abilities? Often they wish their grown child had married someone else.

If we wish our child was something or someone else, we are rejecting what he is. We may wish the best for him, and we may wish him happiness, but to wish he were something different is to say that we do not like what he actually is.

Children don't need this! They need acceptance. That's why wise parents are careful to avoid making comparisons. When we say that another child keeps his room neat or that another child gets his homework done, we're rejecting our child. This doesn't mean we can't insist that our child clean up his room; it *does* mean we dare not use another child as the measuring rod.

Parents need to reject certain types of behavior. Children left to do whatever they want to also feel rejected. However, we can do damage by delivering a message that says, "I wish you were like Allen."

It's easy to establish a pattern of self-rejection by teaching a child to live by comparison. Housing, clothes, activities, grades, and churches may be overdone in an attempt to keep up with other people. Some children are taught to surpass everyone else, but the pressure created by such comparison will bruise the self-esteem.

We know it as keeping up with the Joneses. Children quickly become aware that this is our attitude. They grow up watching our actions but also catching on to our motivations. In many cases they adopt exactly the same set of values. This automatically sentences them to a life of envy and comparison. Few ever escape that trap and free themselves.

One of the most lasting gifts we can give a child is relative freedom from envy (1 Peter 2:1). Almost unlimited opportunities for personal fulfillment and service await those of us who aren't burdened by the tyrant of envy. It's a form of lust which no child needs to inherit (James 4:1,2).

Comparing our children with other children is rejection. Comparing ourselves with others is a form of self-rejection.

All we need to be is ourselves in the hands of a loving God.

Children face enough rejection through outside forces. A parent's great contribution is to assure the child that he is wanted and secure. Normally a child will wonder where he stands unless he is reassured. In a child's life there is plenty of reason to wonder.

A child sees and hears a great deal about abandonment. He knows families that have lost a father through death or other tragedy. The child knows children who live with grandparents, foster parents, or in other arrangements. No one has to introduce the idea of displacement to him; it's all around. Parents do well to reinforce the assurance that the children will not be abandoned.

After attending the funeral of a young mother, my preschool son asked, "What would happen to me if my mother died?" I assured him that I would take care of him. He then asked, "What would happen if you died?"

They need concrete answers to those questions. Our girl asked us if we were ever going to get divorced. The parents of her friend were divorced, and she wanted to know if we would follow suit.

It's an undependable world. A child needs every possible reassurance. To reduce his fear of abandonment is to increase his feelings of security.

A critical time to address this subject is when a second baby is introduced into a family. Many children are confused and hurt by the commotion which surrounds the event.

Practically everyone is ecstatic over the new arrival. Presents are delivered, relatives drop over, and everyone breaks out in jubilation. Few occasions create as much excitement as a new baby.

Meanwhile yesterday's star is pushed into the background. No one is doing flips over him. What could this mean?

Where will the new baby sleep? Will the first child have to give up his bed? There are only three chairs at the table. Will the baby take his chair? Maybe there won't be time or room for the child who was already there.

These are real fears. Those fears turn easily into resentment and severe competition. When not handled well, some children take years to overcome their dislike for a younger child. A few never get over it. They were displaced—rejected—even though it was the furthest thing from their parents' minds.

We can study child-raising practices until we're totally confused. Avoid reading two dozen books with conflicting opinions. However, it does pay to stop and take inventory. We may not be aware of how we are rejecting our children.

To tell a child to sit up at the table is not to reject him. Simply to feel your child isn't trying in school is not to reject him. That may be the fact. More importantly, we need to look for patterns and attitudes within ourselves. Some days we don't enjoy our children. Some days we wish they would hurry up and move out. Those are passing emotions. We need to concern ourselves with deeper patterns.

Do we consistently reject the child? Do we genuinely dislike him? Has he failed to live up to our expectations? Do we think he is responsible for our lost opportunities? Do we imagine that he has hurt our marriage?

In most cases these thoughts are not factual. But we aren't dealing with facts—only with feelings. If we feel these, we place a terrible load on our children and ourselves. By taking inventory, or getting someone to help us, we may be able to isolate the exact problem and deal with it. Parental rejection is a miserable curse for the child—and for the parent.

Watch a child trying to be like his parent. Some make it a point to walk the same way. They want to sit in the same chair. They wear a hat the same way. They dress in aprons and help with the dishes to be like Mother.

Especially in the early years they want to identify closely. That closeness gives them a feeling of security and identification. It helps tell them who they are. When they feel rejected they're pushed away from the identification. They're left to find themselves with no home base. They can't feel safe around their own parents. Young children then face the prospect of finding acceptance in a very scary world.

Another element of strong families is that their members know they can always go home and be accepted. If the world turns hostile, there is always one place they can go to. A rejected child does not have that feeling.

Few parents look a child in the eye and say, "I can't stand you." Rejection usually takes other forms. The parent communicates the fact that he doesn't care by the amount of interest he puts in his child. If he seldom talks to the child, if he avoids playing games, if he is too busy to look at the child's work, the parent is communicating rejection.

A father bought an old house with the intention of fixing it up for resale. Practically every evening and weekend he hung drywall, caulked, and painted. All this time he kept saying it was for his family. He argued that it would teach them that work is important and that you have to sacrifice to get money.

After he sold the house the frustrated dad said, "Never again. I'll tell you what I taught them: I taught them that family isn't important, that children come third or fourth on my list. They learned a lot about greed but little about love."

The tired mother who screams, "I do everything for you kids!" may be doing little for them that matters.

Some parents are uncomfortable with their children. They make them nervous. Children pick that up. They see us smile, talk, even laugh with our peers. But when we are with our children we might tend to freeze up, become edgy, and complain a great deal.

At first children are confused by such conflicting behavior. They hear parents declare how much they care, but they see actions which prove the opposite. When that behavior goes on for some period of time, the child finally and reluctantly figures out what is really happening. Sometimes they understand it before the parents do.

Other children see their parents in a continual plot to get rid of them. "Let's drop the kids here, let's get a babysitter, let's run over there without the children." When that's done at every turn, the child can add it up: Their parents' idea of a good time is to separate from the children.

One child told her parents, "I know what you would like to do most: Get a babysitter and get away from us."

The mad escape from our children may be a form of rejection.

Many parents are able to recognize such actions. They can identify them as reflective of their real feelings or as only a poor pattern which they have not intended. Either way, they can be corrected. Conscientious parents are able to reverse the trend and pull their children close to them. In doing so they may have rescued their children from feelings of rejection.

Fortunately, small children have extraordinary powers of resilience. They can be disappointed and unappreciated during those early years and still snap back with amazing stability. This gives hope to every couple who has had three preschoolers at the same time. Those years are difficult for everyone. In frustration many things are neglected, and often regrettable things are said. As the children enter school, their parents get some breathing room and enjoy their children more.

Mothers who definitely did not want a child frequently change their minds as they are charmed by the infants. Children rebound well from early rejection. Parents should not worry about the spells they have gone through. Most of us get tired of each other sometimes. The pattern over the long haul should be our real concern.

A number of famous parents have rejected their children. The Biblical Jacob is a prime example. He overtly picked out his son Joseph and favored him over the other brothers. Doubtless Joseph was a witty, obedient boy, but Jacob certainly created tremendous animosity between the brothers by preferring one over the others.

In fact he rejected the brothers by accepting Joseph out of proportion (Genesis 37:2-4). Father Jacob has to carry some of the responsibility for driving a wedge between his sons.

Parents can create havoc by rejecting their child or children. They can also spread warmth and stability by the fact of total acceptance. Millions of children have benefited by that feeling of love.

11

Letting Others Down Easy

It usually hurts to be turned down. Each of us has had it happen, and we can remember the pain. We should keep that memory in mind when we need to say no to someone else. Thoughtful rejection is an art. When handled well, it could help lift someone up. If we throw rejection at people like rocks, we will probably injure someone.

The first principle of rejecting others is the Golden Rule: "Do to others as you would have them do to you" (Luke 6:31 NIV). Do we enjoy being crushed, insulted, or yelled at? Do we like to find out about the rejection in a thoughtless, secondhand way? How do we feel when we discover that we've been lied to?

It's a subjective outlook, but it's a good place to start. How would you like to be rejected? After reaching a general conclusion, see if it fits the mix. If it gets the job done and still shows kindness, you probably have the right formula.

When Jesus needed to turn down a former demon-possessed believer, He did it thoughtfully. The man begged to follow Jesus. He was grateful, he seemed dedicated, and his enthusiasm was sincere. However, Jesus told him he could not come. But then He gave the man hope. Jesus told the man to return to his family and be a disciple there, to tell them how much God did for him. The man left, probably with a feeling of disappointment but certainly with a mission, a purpose, a new set of goals (Mark 5:18-20).

We can't handle every situation this well, but we can do well in some.

Many a person has abandoned a promising career because of the way the first few rejections came across. They were such harsh and cruel denunciations that the person went home and packed away his trumpet forever.

Let's consider a few guidelines on how to reject people or their ideas.

Be honest.

Would you like to be lied to? Most of us can be honest without being rude. "Thanks for calling, but I'm busy and I don't want to hear about your product. Better luck at the next place."

That's stating the facts without getting into an unbelievable, indefensible story.

Human beings deserve honest answers, whether they are salesmen, workers, children, spouses, or distributors of religious tracts. Human beings are to be treated with respect, no matter who they are.

Don't make excuses if you have no excuse:

"Thanks for asking, but I'm really not interested."

If you don't want to talk to the religious teams that knock on your door, a straightforward answer will get rid of most of them. But what happens if you give an excuse? They then start to wiggle their way in.

Be crisp, honest, and friendly.

When girls or boys want to turn down dates, they frequently make up excuses. "No, I have a lot of homework." He comes back to ask the next week. Feverishly she digs for another excuse. As hard as it is, the best answer might be, "Thanks for asking, but no thank you."

Be clear.

Don't make people guess what you said. It isn't fair. Why leave both of you hanging? If the person is calling at the wrong time of day, or if you think the product is terrible, or if you are happy with the service you presently have, be specific.

You would enjoy as clear an explanation as possible. So would everyone else.

Years ago I drove a flower delivery truck and met some wonderful people. When calling on one store for the first time, the owner leveled with me. He said that Thursday afternoon was the worst time to call and that the mums were 50 cents too high. But if I could work those two things out, he would look for me again.

It was neat as a tick: I was rejected; I knew why; I knew what needed to be done.

I also remember playing games with managers who gave wild excuses, hid in the back room, or yelled a lot.

Many couples are repeatedly in hot water because they can't say what the problem is. Each spouse is left on his own to resolve some friction he can't comprehend. Clear, precise rejection leaves room for correction and reconciliation.

Be polite.

Every human being is entitled to dignity. If we know what we want to say and will say it distinctly, there is no reason to insult some poor soul trying to make a living.

Much of our harshness and rudeness seems born of insecurity. Afraid we can't stand our ground, we degrade ourselves by being ugly. It's demeaning to both the person we are talking to and to ourselves.

Some people seem to respond best to brisk commands. They refuse to leave or stop calling. The only thing they understand is "Get out"; "Leave"; "Don't come back."

Even with the obnoxious ones, it's good to know you tried to be kind.

Be firm.

Know what you want to say, and say it. If your words indicate one thing and your tone of voice another, you create chaos. Everyone is helped if you think out your answer and give it with conviction.

If a child senses the fact that a parent may not mean it, he knows he can push some more. Put him at rest: "You can't go"; "The door stays open"; "You have to be up by 9:00 A.M." We all function better when our decisions are dependable.

Be flexible.

"Be firm" and "be flexible" sound like contradictions. That's because they are. Life is loaded with paradoxes.

If we are so firm that we can't listen to reason, we border on the boneheaded. There's no need to take a stubborn stand which will work against our own good.

Be encouraging.

If you don't want to burn bridges, make this plain. Tell the person it won't work this time but that you want him to come back.

Let friends know you would like to be invited next time. Be sure the boy understands you would like to be asked again.

Communication means that we let people know where they stand. Rejection tends to stun all of us. If we want the person to return, we need to help him recover from the shock of being turned down. Many people sit alone wishing they had told a friend how much they wanted to be included the next time.

All of us have bad days. Bills come due, our health is poor, our brother-in-law wants to borrow money, we start to get sock rot. Each of us could use a smiling face, a friendly voice, and a bit of gentleness. Since we are all kin, experiencing the same difficulties, we need to let other people down as easily as we would like to be let down ourselves.

Fundamental to being a fellow human being is the need to keep our word. Promises should be given sparingly, but once given our word should become our bond. We should show up because we said we would. Otherwise we are in danger of abusing the human relationship.

Granted, this doesn't have to follow a blind course. If something happens which makes it impossible to carry out your promise, everyone should understand. But under normal circumstances we are bound to do what we have said.

When we can't perform our promise, a phone call and a careful explanation are in order. If we have unreasonably inconvenienced the person, naturally we try to help alleviate the problem.

People are too important to treat shabbily. We need to pledge ourselves to make less promises and keep the valued few we make.

Each of us has a right to know what is going on—especially when it affects our lives. It's cruel to leave other people in confusion because we didn't take time to explain.

Samuel is a good example of a bewildered sufferer. He was crushed when the nation of Israel told him his services were no longer needed. He knew he had done an excellent job. The nation decided they wanted to get rid of their judge, Samuel, and have a king rule them. Samuel folded up in despair. Why did everyone hate him? "After all I have done, that's the thanks I get."

Fortunately, God told Samuel the facts. Israel wasn't rejecting Samuel. Frustrated with their own failures, they were rejecting God Himself. Samuel was merely a representative of God's authority (1 Samuel 8:7).

Samuel had a right to know the facts—honestly,

clearly, and politely. It's too bad the leaders of Israel couldn't have explained it better and saved him some agony.

By letting people down gently we make life a little easier for someone else. We've invested ourselves in helping others in a tough world.

12

Everybody Has
an Opinion

"If you want my opinion, the project is a bunch of junk. I think you're going to cause a lot of headaches for everybody."

With that crisp observation he turned and left the room. He was short, negative, and even rude. The woods are full of highly opinionated people.

The opinionated we will always have with us. They will slice into our plans and leave us bleeding. With little or no help to offer, their only interest is creating havoc. Since this breed of howling monkeys will never go extinct, we need to learn to handle them. We can't let them wreck our projects, our dreams, or our day. Fortunately, even the brick-tossers can be rerouted into positive, constructive forces.

Our first step in gaining control is to become realistic. There aren't nearly as many brick-throwers as we imagine. Most people are polite, cooperative, and encouraging, and would like to see our dreams come true. There is no sense painting an ugly picture of our fellowman when it isn't true.

The real problem is exaggerating the few objectors who actually exist. One negative statement makes us forget 100 encouraging words. If one person praises our project to the point of embarrassment and another person slightly ridicules it, we are likely to remember the second.

This ratio doesn't change the facts: Detractors do populate the area, and we must find some way to make peace with them.

The opinionated aren't asking questions, gathering information, and weighing the facts. You seldom hear them asking about a project. They have a preconceived notion and they're going to tell you about it. You won't have to call them; they'll call you.

If we aren't careful, the opinions of the opinionated will blow us straight out of the saddle.

Since practically everyone has an opinion, it's important to have a general program for processing opinions.

Our first responsibility is to resist opinions. If that sounds strange, weigh the alternatives. By collecting everyone else's two cents we soon turn into putty. We don't know where we stand or if we should stand at all.

A lady said, "I'm against the program; it's too controversial."

That's no reason to throw in the towel. Voices will come from every direction suggesting alternatives, replacements, and color changes. Who needs it? By taking every opinion seriously, we become too bogged down to navigate.

We should be happy to collect real information. The real saints come up and say, "Here's something you might want to consider. Just run it through the hopper and see what you think."

Opinions can be important, and we need to accept some. However, our first inclination must be to sift them. If early auto manufacturers took every opinion seriously, we would still be riding horses. If Wilbur and Orville collected opinions, they would have created an apple cart instead of an airplane.

James was rightfully concerned about Christians who were merely tossed around, doubleminded and unstable (James 1:6-8). One day they believe, the next day they think God is a bullfrog. They gather theories like winter nuts. Don't fall into the trap of trying to allow for everyone and everything.

Develop a natural instinct to resist opinions. When you find an idea you love, determine that you will ride it for all it's worth.

Having said that, I will now say the opposite. Who do you think you are to be above the opinions of other people? While we should resist opinions as a general rule, we shouldn't be so foolish as to totally ignore them. A measure of flexibility is essential to a good dreamer, but instability is deadly. Bees can't pollinate unless they decide on a particular flower.

I had argued against a change in plans we were developing. Lawyers, accountants, and committee members all agreed we were going in the wrong direction. After I resisted the move for a full year, the truth of what they were saying finally dawned on me.

Resist change, but don't ignore the facts. When the facts become too obvious to deny, intelligent change is in order.

Only nerds are above change, but only wimps change every time someone coughs.

Put them together and you have a clear goal which you are willing to refine by making adjustments. From this position you can not only accept opinions, but you can also afford to seek them. You are at the helm in control of your idea, and you are willing to sail the seas with it.

If we seek opinions, we must be honest enough to consider their value. Frequently we ask other people what they think, only to defend what we already believe. It isn't fair.

I asked someone to check my work and tell me what he thought. His reply was, "Do you want me to merely agree with what you have done or do you want me to help improve it?"

A valuable question. Don't involve someone in your work if the involvement isn't honest.

There was an insecure woman who didn't care for a certain person. She asked the individual for his opinion on something he knew little about. He declined at first, but she persisted. Finally he made a couple of weak suggestions. She then felt smug because she had demonstrated that his ideas were inept.

It's a cruel business to seek opinions that we really don't want. To ask for help simply to make ourselves look good flirts with evil.

Look at serious opinions as holding degrees of value. Evaluation helps us escape the extremes. If there is some truth in the idea, we are smart to incorporate it and to thank God that it arrived in time.

When we are crushed by the opinions of others it is usually because we feel a slight change will destroy us. We avoid this by learning to give and take. Give-and-take is a sure sign of maturity.

It's hard to admit that we don't like to give and take. The ability to compromise seems so civilized that we all imagine we do it well.

I remember leaving a businessman's office and thinking to myself, "We both suffer from the same problem—we're dictators." What a miserable thing to admit! It pains me to force my pen to write those words.

However, to accept that fact, if it's true, is to begin reaching out for improvement. Our opinions are not always the best. If I can selectively accumulate educated and uneducated opinions, I may soon be able to pursue better projects. That's a quality well worth opening up to.

Proverbs tells us that a nation falls because of the lack of guidance. But those who seek many advisers make victory a certainty (Proverbs 11:14). That golden premise is tempered by two facts: We must be willing to give our idea definite leadership, and we must refuse to be swayed by every hint of opinion.

A college student said he talked to dozens of friends about picking a future career, and now he was more confused than ever. Naturally! He assumed that everyone else was right, and he was unwilling to grab the problem and take action for himself.

It's no wonder his ship was off-course. The marvel is that it was even afloat!

We become the eternal samplers of opinions. It's like tasting chocolates and musing over the flavors—a lazy man's inactivity.

Thank God for opinions, if not for opinionated people. The views of others—old, young, professional, amateur—are tonics to thirsty souls. Opinions can never rule, but they can help equip a nearly great idea.

13

Feeling Unappreciated

Every parent gets crushed. You break the budget to buy a new coat for your teenager, and there isn't even a hint of a thank you. You prepare a great meal and all you get in return is table talk about the Dallas Cowboys. To top it off, your husband dumps so much catsup on the meat that he wouldn't know if it was cardboard.

Young people get deflated too. They can collect good grades, come in on time, wash the car, put gas in it, and still hear, "Is your room clean?" It's like a knee-jerk reflex with some parents. Anytime there's a lull in the conversation, parents ask if the room is clean.

A lack of appreciation goes with the turf. If we're going to do things with people and for them, we will be unappreciated—not all the time, but enough to make you wonder if it's worth it.

Left unappreciated, we soon feel sorry for ourselves. This leaves us a short step from the stranglehold of self-pity. Self-pity has a way of getting out of control and causing considerable pain.

Instead of being helpless victims of self-pity, we should try to gain the upper hand. To do that we need to know what self-pity is, what causes it, and how we might master some of our feelings.,

A corporation salesperson explained it this way: "I can't win. Last year I met my quota plus an extra 25 percent. How did management react? They raised my quota that much higher for next year. I didn't expect them to give me the company, but I would have liked a small sign of appreciation."

Briefly stated, self-pity is feeling that you're being taken for granted. Consequently, you start to feel sorry for yourself. How deeply you sink into self-pity usually depends on you and your situation.

Practically all of us thrive on some form of acknowledgment. We want to know we count. Strokes are important to keep us going at reasonable performance. Even rats need pellets and seals need fish. To believe we are giving of ourselves for uncaring slobs will turn most of us hostile.

A boss says, "I pay my employees. I don't have to thank them too." Some employers believe they are doing the employees a favor by giving them jobs. Frequently these employers have high rates of turnover because their workers are persuaded that no one cares. Essentially they're correct.

Spouses fall into the same trap. Many leave a relationship simply because they don't feel appreciated. There may be no big fights or dramatic turning points. They merely weren't careful enough to say, "Thank you. That was thoughtful and I love having you around."

Those of us who need strokes should ask ourselves a few important questions. First, is our desire for appreciation within reasonable expectations? Second, have we let people know how much appreciation means to us? Third, can we survive on the nourishment we are now getting?

The first question calls for some personal inventory. Hardly anyone will pat us on the head every time we show up on time. Some of us demand too much in the way of ego massage.

One gentleman has been unable to keep a job because no one can rub his tender soul as much as he needs. Drifting from job to job, he blames everyone else for his inability to stick. We can't expect other people to supply all of our emotional crutches.

We have to become realistic about ourselves. To some extent we need to furnish our own rewards: an evening out, a new coat when we attain certain goals. Pampering ourselves isn't necessarily pagan. Only when it becomes selfishness to the point of thoughtlessness do we have serious conflicts.

Caring for our own emotional needs is sane Christian principle. Paul defended himself. Jesus got away for spiritual renewal. Peter might have benefited from a weekend away once in a while.

Protecting our mental health is no sin.

Try setting your own standards at work. If you type five papers in a row without a mistake, give yourself a special lunch. Should your new sales approach work, take fresh shrimp home to the family. When you increase your productivity by 10 percent, buy a gift for the church.

None of this will eliminate our need for appreciation. However, it will reduce the pressure. Instead of all of our approval coming from undependable sources, we compensate by rewarding ourselves. We lower the intensity by expecting less from others.

If all of this seems simple, remember that there are people who are nearly incapable of rewarding themselves. They don't think they are worth it. Solely dependent on others, they are asking for trouble.

Second, we let people know we could use a little appreciation. Many are unaware of how ungrateful they are.

One approach is to say, "Don't you ever say thank you?" It might get the job done, but it doesn't work on most people.

Maybe a better system is to begin conditioning others to express gratitude. If the person you love needs to give more strokes, you could tell him gently but frankly, "Honey, appreciation means a lot to me. When you tell me I've done something right, it makes me feel great."

That's positive, uplifting, constructive. You didn't tell anyone off; you merely led him along to help strengthen you and your relationship. If your spouse has a brain cell, he should respond to that.

A less direct way is to ask for a general reply. For instance, "Let me know what you think of the pie" invites comment. It's fishing for a compliment, but it subtly leads to a grateful attitude. You want some acknowledgment that you're alive.

The same lead will work with your boss: "Let me

know what you think of this," or, "Is this what you wanted?" or, "This is a little different; let me know how you like it." You are leading the person to deliver what you definitely need. It beats having the boss take your report and walk silently away with barely a grunt.

You're building a protective network. Your expectations have been drawn into a reasonable sphere. You have opened creative arteries to feed your normal need for appreciation.

Third, what happens if you can't survive on the appreciation level you are getting? Suppose you put your best effort out and receive only neglect in return? Some situations are impossible. Having tried to draw approval from your company or boss and failing, you may need to take drastic action. After trying to improve your lot, you may have to move on.

A man worked in a clothing store for a year. During that time he received no raise, no compliments, no promises, no hope. Finally, in despair, he resigned. When he told the boss of his decision, the reply was, "That's a terrible shame. You were one of the best salesmen I've ever had."

How was he to know?

We don't need to *be* appreciated; we need to *feel* appreciated. To appreciate my wife and never tell her has the same effect as not appreciating her. Many people lose a spouse because they failed to show and tell.

Cut off from emotional nourishment, people shrivel up. If we receive no signs of approval we can try to encourage that person to show it or we can produce approval of ourselves as much as possible. Should neither of these work, we may need to look around for a job where appreciation is more likely to be shown.

With such a large number of divorces, many children are painfully confused. A parent says he loves them. However, he fails to call, to come see them, to spend time with them, to go places together. The child fights hard to believe what he is hearing, but he can't reconcile that with what he sees. Therefore love becomes a word with no meaning. It's simply a platitude. If anything, it has an ugly ring.

We don't need to *be* appreciated; we need to *feel* appreciated.

But what if none of this is really our problem? Suppose we receive adequate acknowledgment but still feel unappreciated? Maybe we are victims of self-pity. Unable or unwilling to cope with life as it is, we may have gone too far in feeling sorry for ourselves.

Self-pity isn't created by outside circumstances; it's born within us. Therefore it also must be handled from within.

Each of us should feel a certain amount of compassion for ourselves. Those who don't are lousy survivors in a tough world. If we are terribly hard on ourselves, life becomes a series of bitter pills that are hard to swallow.

The problem arises when compassion for ourselves gets out of hand. We cross the line of healthy caring and enter the world of spoiling ourselves. Spoiling ourselves is to have more compassion than is good for us.

Self-pity means that we are treating ourselves as spoiled brats.

However, we live in a society that's geared to produce its share of self-pity. Instant comparisons lead us to imagine that each of us could have everything. If we buy this hedonistic argument, self-pity is close behind.

I'm referring to the "everybody else is hang-gliding" syndrome. Television leads us to believe that the real essence of life is to sail across the sky without a care and then celebrate the accomplishment with a cool beverage. Those of us who have never driven anything more exciting than a lawn tractor shrivel up in comparison.

If we compare ourselves with everyone else's victories, we are bound to feel sorry for ourselves. Count on it!

Because we've left the world of reality, it's going to be hard to cope. Our first step in countering self-pity is to pull ourselves back into life as it is.

We need to remind ourselves that negatives are part of everyone's experience. Boredom, pain, rejection, isolation, disappointment, and agony are the human condition. Happiness, fulfillment, caring, love, joy, and hope are also part of our lot. Both make up the complete life. To treat every setback as unfair and unbearable leads to extra misery which we definitely don't need.

Look at the complete apostle, Paul. He speaks of the peace of God that passes all understanding (Philippians 4:7). The other side of the coin is that he was beaten, shipwrecked, and stoned, and that he spent at least one night in the open sea

(2 Corinthians 11:25). The peace Paul had was the internal variety. The outside of his life was a shooting gallery.

Have you ever sat around sucking your thumb because you don't have what Paul had? Instead you should be thanking God.

Often the church perpetuates this myth. We are much like the beer commercials: We want people to believe that all Christians are hang-gliding. If they aren't hang-gliding, something must be wrong with them.

With white-toothed smiles we explain how God wants to make you the best seller of corn plaster in the Western hemisphere. All we have to do is trust Him. That might sound good, but we are creating a false impression.

Many of us hunger for more discussion on how to handle grief. We need to know that other Christians have been fired.

Talking with parents about their teenagers has been a frustrating experience. I ask a group what conflicts they have with their young people and receive total silence. If an occasional person ventured a comment it centered on how they were getting along well or how they used to have friction but now are happy as foxes in a chicken coop.

Are we creating self-pity or trying to cure it?

We can't stop self-pity in other people by merely demanding that they grow up. They need to know the facts of what life is actually like. They also need to recognize what they're doing to themselves.

In self-pity we often shut down our senses and look for excuses for our behavior. We persuade ourselves that it isn't our fault or that we can't control it. Once we have transferred the responsibility of our behavior to others, we have entered a dangerous zone of irrational thinking. To claim that other people control our rudder is to say we are helpless.

To fight that false feeling we must accept responsibility for ourselves. If I'm not happy, it's my fault. Anything short of physical incarceration leaves my choices in my own hands. Some of those who have been imprisoned argue that their choice to be happy is still in their own hands.

We are not unhappy because we're broke. We are not unhappy because we're alone. We are not unhappy because no one calls us. We are unhappy because we do not take control of our happiness. To pout and insist that no one loves us ignores the real problem. Why don't we get up and find someone to love? The decision is really ours.

Once we accept this fact, we cease to be victims. Some people ask, "How's life treating you?" The more important question is, "How are you treating life?" We are victims of life if we choose to be.

If we retreat to self-pity we become emotionally crippled. Most of us experience emotions on a wide range. We're happy, silly, elated, mischievous, sad, gloomy, indifferent. When we sulk in self-pity, we chop off the top layer of emotions. We have geared down to a dull drone. Seldom do we leap up to the upper tier.

And why don't we? We are convinced that a gate holds us down, and we believe that this gate was placed there by someone else.

That's what's wrong with our belief system: We put the gate there ourselves, but we blame it on someone else.

What makes this hard to accept is the fact that occasionally someone else removes the gate. He goes out of his way, makes a big fuss over us, shakes our hand, gives us a raise, praises our plaid pants, and sends us straight into ecstasy.

Two days later we're back in the dumper feeling sorry for ourselves. Why? Because we think he dropped the gate again.

We're the only ones who can consistently control our gate. If we want more than a rare glimpse of freedom, we must accept the job of gatekeeper.

Each of us needs to look out for our own mental health. Jesus Christ laid out solid principles that help us keep our heads screwed on right. Forgiveness, love of enemies, prayer, absence of fear, loving one another—each contributes to a balanced personality. A measured amount of self-interest and self-preservation adds to that balance. Self-pity breaks the balance.

Self-pity is self-centeredness. It is not a healthy concern for ourselves. Pouting, moroseness, and thumb-sucking are basically destructive.

Read about Amnon (2 Samuel 13:1-14). He was one of the original nerds. He decided he wanted to have sex with his half-sister. Because he couldn't get what he wanted, Amnon felt sorry for himself. Soon he went into such a serious blue funk that he got sick.

No doubt about it—he believed that other people were making his life miserable. Why couldn't he be gross and violate his sister? Life just wasn't fair.

Giving in to self-pity is flirting with self-centeredness. Self-centeredness gives birth to dangerous behavior. It distorts the concept of ourselves and of other people.

To say this is to admit that practically all of us do it. Read the book of Psalms with an eye open for self-pity. The author is continuously whining over how terrible conditions are. Much of it is complaints over what others have done to him.

He pouts that God has rejected him (60:1). People hate him without reason (69:4). He has to restore things he did not steal (69:4). David isn't the cheery believer riding the crest, oblivious to the trials around him. Understandably, he meets real and imagined enemies. Fortunately, he also finds strength in a God who cares about him (71:12,13).

Often our trouble comes from an either/or approach, as if the bad guys experience self-pity and the good guys are above it. The truth is that we visit both places. Likewise most of us dwell in self-pity for periods of time. Sadly, some of us stay there most of the time.

Talking about self-pity is hard to do but it's frequently helpful. Talking to a friend can help us enunciate what's going on inside us. To tell someone how awful things are might make us realize they aren't so bad after all. The sound of our own voice could bring us to appreciate how well off we are.

At the same time we could gain new insights into how to solve the problem. A friend might suggest some adjustments which would make the situation more acceptable. Some people have been prevented from quitting their jobs because of these little chats. Airing out has saved more than one marriage.

Talks with God have a way of calming us down. He has a way of putting life back into perspective— almost like a voice coming through the stillness saying, "No big deal! Cool it!"

We spend much time trying to live above pain. It's commendable but impossible. A natural goal is to avoid disappointment—but we know it will happen. Tragically, some of us believe we are good enough to escape it all. When pain sneaks in, we become indignant. How did that happen? In response we sink into self-pity because life did not live up to our unrealistic expectations.

Christians are killed, rejected, murdered, thrown out, cheated. They go bankrupt. Christians cannot escape the normal setbacks of life.

A man's job was in jeopardy, and it left him dumbfounded. "How can that happen to me?" he complained. "I go to church, I give, I even read the Bible and pray. You would think God would protect me."

Protect him? From what? Life!

God is more likely to help us through life than He is to help us skirt around it.

As we encounter other people we would do well to remember some fundamentals.

Not everyone is going to appreciate us.

A restaurant served meals to stranded motorists. Half of the people left without offering to pay or saying thank you.

Others cannot send us into the dumps unless we let them.

A man told me he had read one of my books. It was up to me whether his frank comments would send me under the table. They did—until I took hold of myself.

God stays steady as a Rock.

God loves me! How much? Plenty. That love doesn't change according to my moods. Nor does it fluctuate with my activities. When I'm a coward God's love is as firm as a brick and as warm as a blazing hearth (Romans 8:37-39).

It's hard to feel sorry for myself with that kind of love.

14

Thanks for Rejection

There's no sense playing mental games. Some people argue that rejection is really good: It builds character, strengthens resolve, and makes you a better person. That sounds helpful, but why kid ourselves?

Rejection hurts. That's why we call it rejection. Most of the time we want acceptance; that's why we make the proposal. We aren't helped by nonsense that labels mud balls as roses of the future. No need insulting the reader with that baloney!

Isaiah 5:20 has been a tremendous help to me. It taught me that only fools call evil good and good evil. We don't gain anything by washing the outside of dirty cups (Matthew 23:25,26).

Some terrible things have happened because of rejection. I can name a couple of presidential candidates we have rejected who probably would have served much better than the ones we accepted.

I say all of that to try to hold our perspective. Rejection can be horrendous, but it can also be magnificent. It can even be a gift directly from God.

When rejection comes, and the initial shock goes away, we need to stop and ask God if we can be thankful for it.

Let your imagination drift to some of the possibilities.

Many of us can remember a girl who turned us down when we asked her out. It was a wound to our ego. And then to think of the weasel she did go out with!

But there is another side. Today you may be tickled at that memory. What if she had accepted you? You could be married to her. You might have been driven crazy by her highly vocal mother. Years later you have an awkward rejection to thank.

Looking back over my files, I see some book and article manuscripts that were rejected. When I see how pitifully they are written, I become grateful that they were turned down. I wasn't thankful at the time, but some tough editors did us all a favor.

Think of the sleazy places at which you have applied for jobs. What would have happened if they had said yes? You could have worked ten years at a job you thoroughly hated. Rejection can be a genuine friend.

When we survey the "if only's" of our past, most of us will find a few laughs. You tried to buy into a business, but the owners didn't want you. Later, when they went under, you realized how good rejection can be.

Let's celebrate the happiness of rejection! We may not know if God helped us by closing that door, but we can thank Him that the door slammed shut. Thankfulness doesn't have to understand all the forces at work.

A carpenter had a heart attack after 20 years of constant labor. Today he works at a desk job and loves it. He wishes he had found it years ago. His body rejected the hammer and saw. It led to a much more fulfilling career.

We seem to have a need to explain everything. But some actions defy our best reasoning, and that doesn't stop us from being thankful.

Rejection is a school all in itself. For those who care to learn, rejection offers a variety of classes. It teaches us a great deal about ourselves and the way we react to adversity. Through experience it teaches us how to approach people the next time. If we are alert and willing, we will grow after being rejected.

Rejection tells about the world we live in—its demands, its coldness, its standards, its fickleness, its prejudices, its kindness, its paganism, its charm. The way we are turned down gives us three hours of credit in human behavior!

The rejections which are totally destructive are the ones which fail to teach.

Back to the drawing boards. Your next approach will be better planned and executed. We learn from the lumps on our head.

Usually we like to tell stories of grandeur, of athletic feats too marvelous to imagine. We might help more people by sharing some of our setbacks. What did they do to us and how did we cope with them? These stories help most of us handle life as we face it.

The Christian gift in the middle of rejection is the spirit of thankfulness. For it to be a gift of deliverance it must be understood correctly. Thankfulness doesn't come easily in hardship, but it can be a reality.

We can't always be thankful for the rejection itself. If we reason this out, we see some of the folly. To say we're thankful for the Holocaust of the Jews defies sanity. How can we say it was good that countries did not send food to starving Ethiopians? Faith doesn't ask us to abandon common sense. Some rejection is terrible.

It's not an act of faith to accept every horror as if it were a royal wedding.

The trick is to find things to be thankful for when the ceiling is falling in. When we are fired, we still thank God for our family, our health, our good friends. That's what Paul meant when he told us to be thankful in all things (1 Thessalonians 5:18; Ephesians 5:20).

Not everything that happens to us is the perfect will of God. That's fatalism. Why make decisions? Why avoid accidents? Why take medicine? If each event is personally packaged by our heavenly Father, our actions are of no consequence.

The will of God is to find something to be thankful for in all situations. That doesn't make each situation good.

This is God's protection against bitterness. If every rejection wrecks our outlook on life, we soon turn cynical and twisted. Taken to the extreme, many murderers, arsonists, and rapists had trouble working through their rejection. She turned him down for another man, so he shot her. He was ejected from a restaurant for being loud. Unable to put it to rest, he torched the place, killing 24 people. People who can find only bitterness are courting further harm to themselves or to others.

A friend recently lost his job. He was considering other options when the axe fell. It hurt to be let go. If they were going to part company, he would rather have had the privilege of resigning. But it didn't happen. The pink slip won out.

Immediately he began investigating the exciting opportunities he had been dreaming of. As he thought about it, he realized how fortunate he was.

In a list of best choices, he could have weighed his opportunities while he still had a job. Without a job he was forced to choose, and possibly the pressure made the decision-making a little more difficult. Maybe it also caused him to make up his mind where otherwise he might have drifted in pointless employment.

He doesn't have to know which one would have been better. More important, he can thank God for where he is, for what he has, and for where he is going.

Some rejection turns out beautifully, and we can thank God for it. Other rejection is ugly, but we can thank God for other things. Either way, we escape bitterness and rise to a bright tomorrow.

15

Rejection As Building Blocks

You ask farmers if they are finished harvesting and bankers if interest rates are going to come down. What do people ask writers? "What are you working on?" When I tell them it's a book on rejection, practically everyone gives an immediate reaction: "I need that."

Parents, teachers, ministers, young people, store clerks, doctors, and lawyers each say the same thing: "I would appreciate some help." Rejection is real to them, and it is painful. Most of them feel it does much harm and little good.

Carefully, without stretching reality, we need to ask how we can turn rejection into an asset. How can we make it work for us? It's like the doctor who made a minor misdiagnosis. He said he couldn't do anything about the mistake. The question was how it could help him do a better job next time.

Many of us think we have learned from rejection when we haven't. We then go on to make the same mistake at the next job. We wade into the second marriage with the same sharp bristles we wore in the first. The high percentage of divorces in second marriages testifies that rejection by itself is not a good teacher.

However, rejection which leads to solid reassessment is a master instructor.

Once we say we would like to learn from the rejection we have faced, we're halfway home: We've decided to not drown in self-pity.

Rejection is no reflection on our self-worth. We may have failed. However, that doesn't make us failures. Failing is an act. Failure is a condition. All of us are the first; none of us is the second.

If we will turn rejection into building blocks, we can make ourselves stronger.

Building Block Number One

Rejection is a great chance to reevaluate ourselves. Thank God for the opportunity! You could sell newspapers the rest of your life, but if a couple of large dogs would run you out of their yards, you might be forced to take a serious look at your job.

Questions like "What am I doing?" "Where am I going?" and "Am I happy where I am?" are quizzes worth taking. And we might not take them until that huge German shepherd comes tearing around the garage.

Even deeper questions call out for answers. Maybe our personality could use an overhaul. Are you telling fifth-grade jokes to adults? Do you monopolize a conversation? Do you think your gift is to find the fault in other people?

People can and do change their personalities. Startled by what they see in themselves, they

consciously alter their behavior. They begin center-
ing their conversations on other people. They
keep their paragraphs short and let others join in.
They make a point to laugh at the jokes that others
tell.

Not content to be victims, they take serious inventory. Friends can offer a few suggestions.
Spouses are excellent at giving assistance; unfortunately, most of us don't care to listen.

When you are rejected, that rejection can
become a solid block in the wall of life you are
constructing.

Jesus was a rejected stone. In the imagery He
was thrown away, unfit to be a part of the building.
God took the rejected stone and made Him the
cornerstone (Matthew 21:42). He became the most
important stone in the structure; the rejected stone
became the building block.

When we are careful to knock off a few rough
edges, rejection can become a valuable part of our
building too. We take time to look it over and ask
what needs to be done to turn it into an asset.

Building Block Number Two

A few sharp rejections will probably turn most of
us into sensitive, caring people. But it doesn't happen automatically. Rejection seems to leave some
people callous and mean. The choice is ours. To
go the wrong way is to enter the dungeon of warped
personality.

Anyone who has been chewed out unfairly can
remember the sting. You can still feel your blood
percolate as you listened to a tirade about things
you didn't do. Turn it into a building block. Make

yourself a better person because you learned that pain is no fun.

Hopefully we will remember this when we talk to our children. We will handle them with sensitivity. They are easily mistreated. They are quickly crushed. Because we recall the pain of being crushed, we refrain from hurting them.

The Bible tells us that Jesus knew the pain of being tempted. Because He experienced temptation, He can help us when we face it (Hebrews 2:18). Bad experiences make great building blocks.

When it becomes our responsibility to fire someone, we will do it with consideration because we've been there ourselves. If we need to tell someone his handcrafted wooden hats won't sell, we will do it without killing his love to create.

Kindness is a gift. Most of us receive it by watching kindness in other people or by observing cruelty and promising we will never repeat it.

Building Block Number Three

Rejection is responsible for millions of talks with God. When a person feels like he's been kicked in the stomach, when his eyes water and his throat is as tight as a brick, he has a great reason to pull close to God and get to know Him a bit better.

There's nothing to be ashamed of if a person goes to God more often under pressure. Though He'd like to hear from us regularly, He won't shut us off when the bottom is dropping out. Unlike human beings, He avoids fits of moodiness. Rejection is an excellent reason to visit with God.

Talking with God has a way of putting rejection back into perspective. To have been turned down at the local clothing store becomes merely one stone on a long highway. While it's important, it isn't vital. One rejection is painful but not terminal. Conversations with God have a way of reducing setbacks to their proper size.

They bring tension under control. Not only have you been able to talk to Someone, but you went straight to the top. Venting is mentally healthy when it's done correctly.

Bringing rejection to God is more than a psychological lift; it's putting the matter into the hands of Someone who can bring action. This doesn't mean He has to; God isn't a pen that must write every time or we throw it away. God may conclude that the rejection you face is good in its context. There could be overriding factors that none of us understand.

Possibly God will move mountains. Maybe the mountain that needs to be moved is us. We might never be the same after wrestling through rejection with our heavenly Father.

Hardship can do for us what prosperity can never touch. If rejection brings us closer to God, it can be a profitable experience.

Building Block Number Four

Any encounter which gives us a sense of humility has to be beneficial. Many of us have become insane with distorted estimates of our own ability. Self-esteem gone to seed results in unbearable arrogance.

We attend seminars and listen to pep talks designed to give us enormous self-confidence. These rallies are a great help to motivate and stimulate us. They are also ego trips that can give us bloated misconceptions of ourselves and of others.

Rejection has a way of landing most hot-air balloons. And it does so with a thump.

The Bible has an objective view on humility. It tells us to avoid thinking of ourselves more highly than we ought (Romans 12:3). But without skipping a beat, it goes on in the next set of verses to outline our gifts (Romans 12:4-8).

We are surrounded by extremes. One group shouts that Christians can do anything. Reportedly our only problem is the failure to dream big for God. The other group says we are all worms. There is nothing good that we can ever do.

As is often the case, truth lies in the middle. The Biblical view of man will not permit arrogance nor will it allow self-defacing.

Rejection serves as a safety valve. When we become overly impressed with ourselves, a kick in the shorts brings us back to earth. It's an attitude adjuster. We can be thankful it comes along when we need it.

Reasonable humility is a Christian virtue (Colossians 3:12). It reminds us that we are no better than the sick, the hungry, the illiterate, the prostitute. We may be different, but we are no better.

Without rejection many of us begin to feel invincible. Knots on our heads are sometimes more valuable than crowns.

Building Block Number Five

The good thing about a trash heap is that you can stand on top and see farther. Losers are buried under the trash; winners climb to the top.

If we never experience rejection, we miss a great many opportunities. Being set back gives us the chance to reevaluate, redirect, and rise higher.

How many people have gone on to fantastic careers because they failed an entrance exam? They had a door slammed in their face only to discover a better one open.

Failure is failure. It doesn't help to redefine the term. But failure is also a platinum opportunity for us to rise up to better things.

One study found that of people who became millionaires, a large number had gone bankrupt at some time. They weren't immune to failure; they simply knew how to bounce back.

Often when I hear about a pastor who is leading a huge congregation, I wonder about the former churches he served. No doubt some of those seemed like failures. But he learned. He adjusted. He stepped up.

Charlie Shedd is an excellent writer. He has several million sellers and enjoys the admiration of many people. Yet his first couple of books on church administration were not blockbusters. But he learned. He adjusted. He stepped up.

If rejection merely teaches us how to handle rejection, it's not enough. Simply learning to take a punch won't prove helpful. It is only when we use rejection as a stepping-stone that we turn it into a shining gem.

I have a friend who hates to fail. When he is rejected either personally or professionally, he is jolted at first, like everyone else. After the initial shock he sets his feet and gains his balance. Determined to gain from the experience, Dave asks what set him back and how he can improve the situation, and then he charges ahead. By remaining level-headed he bounces back stronger than before. Dave keeps growing through life.

After a tough day it's fun to sit in a hot tub and read a book. If you're lucky you will catch it each time you doze off. Usually I stand the book on the floor when I finish reading.

Last night everything worked fine as I repeated this lazy man's ritual. However, when I picked up the book it was wet—a 17-dollar library book was wet!

Immediately I started huffing and puffing because I didn't want to fork out that kind of money. I acted and sounded like someone had hidden my teddy bear.

Later my wife, Pat, cut through to the core of the problem by saying, "It only proves you're human."

Exactly. I didn't want to be human. I thought I should be above mistakes. But the fact was that I messed up. Yet there was no need to reject myself. I will pay for the book, and next time I'll be more careful.

That's growing and adjusting.

Other Books by William L. Coleman:

Courageous Christians	David C. Cook
Getting Ready For My First Day at School	Bethany House
Listen to the Animals	Bethany House
Making TV Work for Your Family	Bethany House
My Magnificent Machine	Bethany House
Peter: You Are My Rock	Harvest House
The Great Date Wait	Bethany House
Today I Feel Like a Warm Fuzzy	Bethany House
Today I Feel Loved	Bethany House
You Can Be Creative	Harvest House